D0888098

hope deferred

hope deferred

Heart-Healing Reflections on Reproductive Loss

NADINE PENCE FRANTZ AND MARY T. STIMMING, EDITORS

Contributors

Nadine Pence Frantz

Serene Jones

Kristen E. Kvam

Linda A. Mercadante

Mary T. Stimming

THE PILGRIM PRESS CLEVELAND, OHIO

DEDICATION

*For those
who mourn
empty wombs
and empty arms —
may your hearts
be made glad.*

The Pilgrim Press, 700 Prospect Avenue, Cleveland, Ohio 44115-1100
thepilgrimpress.com
© 2005 by Nadine Pence Frantz and Mary T. Stimming

All rights reserved. Published 2005

Biblical quotations are primarily from the New Revised Standard Version
of the Bible. © 1989 by the Division of Christian Education of the National
Council of the Churches of Christ in the U.S.A., and are used by permission.

Printed in the United States of America on acid-free paper

10   09   08   07   06   05   5   4   3   2   1

Library of Congress Cataloging-in-Publication Data

Hope deferred: heart-healing reflections on reproductive loss /
   Nadine Pence Frantz and Mary T. Stimming, editors ; contributors,
   Nadine Pence Frantz . . . [et al].
       p.   cm.
   Includes bibliographical references and index.
   ISBN 0-8298-1617-8 (alk. paper)
       1. Consolation.   2. Miscarriage—Religious aspects—Christianity.
3. Infants (Premature)—Death—Religious aspects—Christianity.
4. Bereavement—Religious aspects—Christianity.   I. Frantz, Nadine Pence,
1953–   II. Stimming, Mary T. (Mary Theresa)

BV4907.H65   2005
242'.4—dc22

2005047625

contents

FOREWORD

Infertility: could it ever be considered a *gift?* Poison and a curse —that's how this unexplained infertility of ours felt to me for what seemed like an eternity. Month after month, nine years of trying to have a child of our own was like having to drink bitter waters from a poisoned well. Nothing could break the sinister hold of barrenness on our lives, not strict adherence to whatever expert advice we could get, not prayer, not the latest infertility techniques, not fasting, nothing. One hundred months' worth of hopes, all dashed against the stubborn realities of bodies that just wouldn't produce offspring. At times, like Abraham, we hoped against hope, and yet the God "who gives life to the dead and calls into existence the things that do not exist" (Rom. 4:17) wouldn't help our bodies give us an Isaac of our own.

Christian community wasn't much help either. Every time we would go to worship, the laughter and boisterousness of the little ones milling around in the community room would remind me of unfulfilled dreams. The season of Advent was the worst. "For unto us a child is born, unto us a son is given," I would hear read or sung in hundreds of different variations. But from me a child was withheld. The miracle of Mary's conception, the rejoicing of the heavens at her newborn child, the exultation of Elizabeth, all became signs of God's painful absence, not God's advent. "And the government shall be upon his shoulder . . ." If God's Son indeed was in charge, it seemed that he didn't care to move even his royal finger in our favor. At Christmas, I felt like a child in a large family, the only one to whom parents had forgotten to give gifts. Others' joy increased my sadness. "And his name shall be called, Wonderful, Counsellor, the mighty God . . ." (Isa. 9:6 KJV). No, not wonderful; at best puzzling. No, not a mighty God; at best, a sympathetic but disappointing divine observer.

Then, in a maternity ward in Chino, California, came the absolutely unforgettable moment when a nurse rolled two-day-old Nathanael into the room of Lisa, his birth mother. She took him into her arms, embraced him lovingly for a moment, and then gave him to us to be our own—the most incredible of gifts! A few years later, Michelle let my wife Judy witness the miracle of birth; the birth of Michelle's own flesh and blood, Aaron, whom she gave to us as our son. Nathanael was then four. Later that day, he, as the tender and awestruck big brother, cradled tiny Aaron in his arms. As I watched them, my joy as a father was complete.

It was only as I was reading the essays of this book that I realized the significance of that joy. During those nine years of infertility I wasn't waiting for a child who stubbornly refused to come. That's what I thought at the time. But in fact, I was waiting for the two boys I now have, Nathanael and Aaron. I love them, and I want them in their unsubstitutable particularity, not children in general of which they happened to be exemplars.

Then it dawned on me: Fertility would have robbed me of my boys. From my present vantage point, that would have been a disaster—the disaster of not having what I so passionately love. Infertility was the condition for the possibility of these two indescribable gifts. And understanding that changed my attitude toward infertility. Since it gave me what I now can't imagine living without, poison was transmuted into a gift, God's strange gift. The pain of it remains, of course. But the poison is gone. Nine years of desperate trying was like one long, painful childbirth, the purpose of which was to give us Nathanael and Aaron. True, had we had biological children of our own, I would have loved and wanted them, and I would have been spared the pain. But that's what would have happened. It didn't. I have Nathanael and Aaron. They are whom I love. They are whom I want. And it's they who redeem the arduous path that led to having them.

Infertility as a painful but welcome gift—that's my experience with reproductive loss. Others have had different experiences. I am a man, and a woman's experience might have been different from mine; Judy's certainly was and continues to be. Others may have eventually had a child who was biologically their own. They may have decided that they shouldn't have children and proceeded to live happily as a couple. They may have adopted children yet still continued to long for flesh from their flesh and bone from their bone. They may still mourn the pain of infertility or stillbirth as an irretrievable loss that no child who came later could redeem. I don't want to suggest that my experience is in any way exemplary. It's simply an experience that shows one possible way of redeeming a terrible loss.

The five extraordinary essays that comprise the book *Hope Deferred* all come at the problem of reproductive loss from slightly different angles. Though none describes an experience quite like my own, I've been moved by each of them. I was moved partly because I know the authors, and I know some of their pain. I was one of the fifteen participants at the consultation on teaching at the Wabash Center for Teaching and Learning in Theology and Religion at which the idea for the book was born. At the time, Judy and I were at a low point in our struggle with infertility. But mainly I've been moved by these fine essays because they are so close to life, its pains and joys, its dashed hopes and fulfilled dreams. This is theology at its best, in the midst of life, employing the rich resources of the Christian faith to grapple insightfully and passionately with the raw stuff of our fragile natality.

Miroslav Volf
Director, Yale Center for Faith and Culture
Henry B. Wright Professor of Theology

ACKNOWLEDGMENTS

This project began under the auspices of the Wabash Center for Teaching and Learning in Theology and Religion. In particular, we are indebted to Lucinda Huffaker, William Placher, and Raymond Williams for their early encouragement of our work together. There is something strangely fitting in this book's inception at a center located at an all-male college.

We are grateful to James Lewis and the Louisville Institute for the generous support provided through two grants. Given our subject matter and the fact that during the production of this text there were nine children among us, we are especially appreciative of Louisville's underwriting of the childcare required for us to do our work. We also are grateful to our respective institutions, Bethany

Theological Seminary, Yale Divinity School, Saint Paul School of Theology, Methodist Theological School in Ohio, and Dominican University, for their assistance and encouragement in this project.

During the final stages of this project, we were graced by the skills of two fine editors. Harriet A. Ziegler proved that copy editors could be exacting without being exasperating, and Kim Sadler of The Pilgrim Press proved that intellectual concerns and practical considerations could work together for the greater good.

Finally, we offer our deepest gratitude to our families and friends. Amidst life's disappointments and sorrows, they make our hearts glad.

PERMISSIONS

"The Sitting Time," by Joe Digman from *When Hello Means Goodbye: A Guide for Parents Whose Child Dies before Birth, at Birth or Shortly after Birth* by Pat Schwiebert and Paul Kirk, Perinatal Loss Project staff, 1981, 1985, 1993. Used by permission of Perinatal Loss. ▪ "Otwock VII," by Kadya Molodowsky from *Paper Bridges: Selected Poems of Kadya Molodowsky.* Translated and edited by Kathryn Hellerstein, Wayne State University Press, 1999. Used by permission of Kathryn Hellerstein. ▪ "A Flower and Not a Flower," by Po Chu-I. Translated from the Chinese by Duncan Mackintosh. All reasonable efforts were made to contact Mr. Mackintosh through Routledge & Kegan Paul Ltd., Vanderbilt University Press, and public records, to no avail. ▪ "Comfort for Women Who Have Had a Miscarriage," by Martin Luther, reprinted from *Luther's Works,* Vol. 43, edited by Gustav K. Wieneke, copyright © 1968 Fortress Press. Used by permission of Augsburg Fortress. ▪ "Lament Psalm Forty-Seven," by Ann Weems from *Psalms of Lament.* ©1995 Ann Barr Weems. Used by permission of Westminster John Knox Press. Not to be duplicated without written permission from Westminster John Knox Press, 100 Witherspoon Street, Louisville, KY 40202.

Hope deferred makes the heart sick.

—Proverbs 13:12

INTRODUCTION *longing*

GATHERING

We were among fifteen theologians at a consultation on teaching called by the Wabash Center for Teaching and Learning in Theology and Religion in Crawfordsville, Indiana. For three days we had been talking about our teaching goals, our syllabi and assignments, our institution's support or lack of support of theology, and the current state of the discipline. At various points small groups had met, but on the fourth day, for the first time, the small group happened to be the five of us, the only women at the consultation. Our small group conversation on institutional support of our teaching quickly turned to comparisons of maternity benefits, child-care options, and the ways our institutions did or did not take into account our status as mothers or single parents.

But it wasn't until we were in the women's room later on that day that the institutional talk dropped away and one woman gently said to another, "I'm very sorry to hear of your recent miscarriage. I lost a child at six months and I know it is very hard." Attention to task stopped, and soon we were leaning on the sinks and against the stall doors, talking about our lives. We stood together in that closed, private space and shared about desire, birth, death, and loss.

In several respects, we were an atypical group of female theologians. All five of us were either married or once married, all of us had sought to be mothers, and all of us had miscarried. Each of us had lost a child through miscarriage or early delivery, a fact that is striking. Three of us struggled with long-term infertility, two had lost children in the second trimester, two had adopted children, one was in the process of adoption, and two had children by birth. Not the usual population statistics, but parts of women's lives that are more common than is often acknowledged.

From that initial gathering in the women's room in 1996, our collaborative work expanded and took shape. We began meeting as we could, once or twice a year, pouring out our stories and naming with each other the theological questions they evoked. We listened to each other and noted what was common in our experiences of infertility, miscarriage, and stillbirth, and we noted what was particular to each of our situations. As we started to put our reflections in writing, we shared our work with each other for response and further refinement. Over time, many of the individual threads that we shared became woven into this collective work.

As we talked with each other, we also talked with others about such experiences. There were many reminders over the years of friends and relations who also grieved reproductive losses and who struggled to make sense of them in light of their understandings of God and the Christian life.

CHILDLESS IN AMERICA

According to the American Society for Reproductive Medicine, 6.1 million Americans currently experience infertility, which is 10 percent of the childbearing population. Additionally, 25 percent of women of childbearing age will experience a miscarriage, and one in eighty pregnancies will end in a stillbirth. Infertility, miscarriage, and stillbirth are sadly widespread. A collective term for infertility, miscarriage, and stillbirth is hard to come by. "Pregnancy loss" won't work because it excludes infertility. We use "reproductive loss" although we are aware of its limitations. There are forms of reproductive loss that don't fall neatly into these three types. But for our purposes, we will employ this term to refer to the three forms of loss we experienced and seek to explore theologically.

The reproductive losses at the heart of this volume concern the inability to have desired biological children and the miscarriage of a hoped-for child. Thus, we do not address the experience of abortion. Although many women mourn after an abortion, their sorrow does not include distress over the failure of their body either to conceive or carry a pregnancy. Circumstances can lead women to terminate wanted pregnancies but this is not the type of loss considered here. Arguably, the lines of distinction between this and the experiences of infertility, miscarriage, and stillbirth are more conceptually than existentially precise, but this lies beyond the scope of this work.

In clinical terms, infertility describes a biological condition in which conception cannot take place. Its definition is often expanded to include biological conditions in which a fertilized egg cannot be sustained *in utero* for any number of reasons, including genetic ones. A miscarriage (in medical terms a "spontaneous abortion") is the loss of a pregnancy after conception but before twenty-four weeks. Stillbirth is the loss of a pregnancy any time from twenty-four weeks to term, in which the fetus dies *in utero* or

3

immediately following delivery. In many such cases, the fetus must be delivered either by cesarean or vaginal birth, hence the term "stillbirth." These definitions work reasonably well for the medical profession. The terms distinguish and name various ways the reproductive system is thwarted in its fulfillment.

But biological facts alone did not qualify these experiences to be the objects of our reflection in the women's room that summer day in Indiana. Personal and cultural narratives invest biological events with meaning. As we poured forth our stories of longing and loss, we recognized the powerful role certain aspects of American life had in shaping our reactions to our reproductive struggles. We recognized that becoming a mother through adoption was generally viewed as "second best" and living without parenting was viewed with even deeper suspicion. Recognizing this social mediation became a source of solace for us because it helped us name the many false bases of our senses of personal failure and inadequacy. Such recognition also helped open our eyes to Christian affirmations that push against the cultural narratives of blame and failure.

Despite feminism's efforts, the dominant contemporary script for women in America is to be wife and biological mother. We recognize that the identification of women with mothering is neither unique to American culture nor to our times, yet it is the time and culture in which we live. Writer Laurie Lisle contends that the role of the social mother was highly valued prior to the Civil War, even more highly than that of the biological mother. Nonetheless, there persists to this day a view that "maternity is necessary for female maturity."[1] When childlessness in America reached 27 percent during the period between 1885 and 1915, a systematic campaign began against single women and nonmaternal wives as "unfulfilled and incomplete." Even leaders of the early women's movement, themselves often single and childless, argued motherhood was central to women's identity. Hostility towards the childless around the turn of the twentieth century was exacerbated by the white "race suicide" panic sparked by the fall of the birthrate among white Anglo-Saxon Protestant women and its rise among other "less desirable" groups.[2]

Social historian Elaine Tyler May, who has charted American reproductive history, suggests that in some respects it is more painful to be childless in America now than in earlier eras:

> Although childlessness has always carried a stigma, the stakes in having children have evolved over time. For centuries, the American national identity has been connected to its fertility. . . . This concern about proper procreation found expression in a number of experiments in reproductive engineering during the nineteenth century. . . . In this context, the meaning of childlessness changed from a matter of community survival to a question of civic virtue. . . . For the first time, infertility emerged as a serious problem facing the nation, and voluntary childlessness became a crime against the citizenry. . . . But it was not until after World War II that reproduction became a national obsession, and childlessness a unique identity. . . . The fierce pronatalism of the babyboom years marked infertility as profoundly tragic and voluntary childlessness as downright subversive.[3]

The post–World War II period has also brought two key technological changes that affect the American experience of childlessness. First came the development and widespread use of the birth control pill. As infertility and adoption educator Patricia Irwin Johnson notes, the success of the pill in preventing conception has contributed to a view of reproduction as something one controls, something one can turn off or on at will.[4] This more mechanized model of reproduction fuels women's rage at their inability to "make" their bodies pregnant. Mistakenly thinking that they can actualize their reproductive capacity as easily as they can suppress it, contemporary American women are often baffled by this encounter with human limits. Reproduction is often perceived as a task on par with any other human endeavor, even the most mundane. A recent craft magazine ad has a softly lit picture of a sleeping infant with the accompanying text: "You made her, you can make a cross-stitch." Madison Avenue's failure to detect a difference between having a baby and stitching a pattern reinforces and reflects an American view of reproduction as something we, particularly women, "do."

Second, the advent and increased accessibility of new artificial reproductive technologies (ART) encourages women to pursue biological parenthood to extremes never before contemplated. The successes of ART, albeit statistically less impressive than are often claimed, have dramatically raised women's expectations for pregnancy and childbirth.[5] The infertility clinic culture promotes the promise that the medical world can solve most, if not all, reproductive problems if only women will work hard and stick with it long enough. The fact that ending infertility treatment is called "quitting" speaks volumes.

Intensifying the effects of these technological changes is our culture's increased tendency to value people primarily in economic terms. Individuals as well as corporations are described and measured in terms of what we "produce" or "make," be it through the labor of body or of mind. In such a culture, to experience our body as "unproductive" is to experience our body as a social failure. It also runs counter to the naïve American optimism that "if you can dream it, you can do it." We have come to expect that we should be able to achieve the particular future of our desiring. A consciousness of the limits within which we forge our path is weak at best.

Each of these factors becomes a thread in our culture's message to women. Few women would disagree with Elizabeth Barthelot's claim that "women are taught from birth that their identities are inextricably linked with their capacity for pregnancy and childbirth and this is inextricably linked with mothering."[6] To grow up a "woman" in this culture is to grow up formed by a script wherein one's body is assessed in terms of its capacity to give life and thereby to make one "a mother." Depending on one's social location, this script takes different forms (often theological ones) and thus affects women's self-understanding in different ways and to varying degrees. But even in the context of these differences, the force of this construction is strong, its pull virtually inescapable. Many women now have social permission to resist this pull because of the advances of feminism. Even in such cases, however, its power remains, if only at the level of unconscious expectations that are continually reinforced by dominant social and theological images of women as mothers.

The cultural definition of women in terms of their maternal status is immense in its power to coerce and shame. Many infertile women describe their experience as one of "not being a real woman," or of "being on the outside looking in." The extent to which they feel inadequate or like outsiders is in part a measure of the weight the culture has put on motherhood.[7] Infertile men report such self-evaluations, but at a much lower rate. This equation of female worth and being a mother undergirds much of the despair regarding infertility, miscarriage, and stillbirth.[8] One of the goals of our essays is, from a Christian perspective, to challenge and debunk the equation of biological motherhood with female worth. In various ways, the chapters that follow explore resources of the Christian tradition that offer comfort and corrective to the self-destructive narrative of women enduring reproductive loss. They offer an expanded vision of what it means to be female, to be human, and to be a child of God.

While all the essays are attentive to this dimension of the grief occasioned by reproductive loss, certain elements of the infertility and miscarriage experience appear only in individual chapters. It is increasingly clear that the loss experienced in infertility, miscarriage, and stillbirth is multiple and layered. Those supporting someone through these crises often presume that their suffering is occasioned by the obvious lack of a desired child, but research supports Maggie Kirkman's contention that these losses are complex. Kirkman speaks of "the loss of identity as a mother, of children who exist only in the autobiographical narrative, of relationships with those children and grandchildren, of hopes and dreams of the future, of participation in the world of mothers, of acknowledgement by society as fully developed women, [and] of a genetic future" as identifiable losses that complicate the grief process.[9]

Readers will notice that our essays vary as to which of these losses are at the heart of our reflections. For example, "Why" centers on the loss of autobiographical narrative and the hopes and dreams contained within a marriage; "Sorrow" highlights the loss of the physical realities of pregnancy and the participation in the world of mothers; "Rupture" explores the loss of control over the self and of the hopes and dreams of the future; "Comfort" ponders a loss of relationship; and "Faith" considers the loss of a jointly conceived, genetically linked child. Thus our personal stories lead us to privilege some types of loss over others. It is our hope that together the five essays cover a wide portion of the spectrum of responses to reproductive loss, and hence will be of interest to a broad variety of readers.

THEOLOGY

During our initial conversations in Indiana, we shared the titles of many fine works of sociology and psychology available that document the myriad effects of infertility and miscarriage (see bibliography under *Reproductive Loss: Infertility, Miscarriage, and Stillbirth*). But we were hard-pressed to name any *theological* works explicitly devoted to our experiences. In the course of our conversations, we spoke of struggles with prayer, of painful treatment within our churches, of anger with God and others, of being unable to speak of God coherently, and of other theological wrestling, but in our searches for wisdom we had not encountered any serious, sustained theological reflections on such topics in direct connection with infertility, miscarriage, and stillbirth.

Several of us sighed over the spiritual tracts well-meaning family and friends had sent our way. They were a comfort of sorts—insofar as they at least recognized the depths of our sorrows—but, in general, they were completely removed from modern understandings of theological thought. Their use of scripture was reductionistic and their understandings of key theological terms such as providence and creation were grounded in pre-Enlightenment assumptions.

Others expressed their disappointment in the lack of attention to these experiences among contemporary feminist writings. A few spoke appreciatively of nontheological works that devoted a chapter or a portion thereof to "religious or spiritual" concerns. But again, there were serious limits to these. Too often they were very short treatments of complex matters and their authors, though adequate, were usually untrained in theology. Some works by Jewish authors were mentioned approvingly as models of what we sought, but no one was aware of the existence of such a work from the Christian tradition. The best we could come up with were brief articles by pastors and theologians (see bibliography under *Pastoral Care and Grief Counseling*). Our frustration became part of the impetus of this project.

Given the deeply personal roots of this volume, it embodies our concerns and our biases. Although we prize the diversity of Christian traditions we represent (Church of the Brethren, Disciples of Christ, Lutheran, Presbyterian, and Roman Catholic), we are aware that we are all white, middle-class, married or once-married women. As we each know fellow theologians with divergent social profiles who had also grieved reproductive losses, we debated inviting them to contribute. Over time, however, the uniqueness of our bond, the extent of our collaborative work, and the exigencies of publishing dissuaded us from expanding our circle. We believe that our friends' stories informed our reflections and that their unique voices will be heard in other forums as well. We are also aware that our common vocation as systematic theologians has resulted in the lack of a sustained reflection drawing from the Christian scriptures and of a sustained treatment of pastoral and liturgical considerations. Given our own particular scholarly gifts, these are topics that must be left to others.

We wish this could be a book that sets to rest all the questions that arise for individuals and couples struggling to discern what God is doing and saying in their suffering. Alas, such an enterprise is beyond us, perhaps even beyond human understanding. Instead we hope to think through, to put into conversation with the texts and practices of our tradition, our own stories and practices. That is, to us, what it means to do theology. For it is our theological conviction that our experiences inform and help us understand the confessions and beliefs of our Christian faith and that the resources and traditions of the Christian faith help us understand our own stories. Both inform, challenge, and illuminate each other. This conversation is the reflective process of theology, and its task is not done until both sides of the conversation are fully examined in light of the other.[10]

The strength of this manner of doing theology is that it refuses to solidify theology into a set of objective and universal propositions sealed against ongoing discernment. The weaknesses of this approach are inattentiveness to stories other than our own and overattentiveness to contemporary experience without sufficient attention to scripture and tradition. We have sought to avoid these by becoming familiar with others' experiences of reproductive loss and through sustained engagement with some of the classic thinkers and texts of Christian theology. Two of the articles do this explicitly: "Sorrow" gains insight from the work of Thomas Aquinas (ca. 1225–74), and "Comfort" centers on a tract by Martin Luther (1483–1546). "Why" and "Faith" use this method in relation to a wider sweep of Christian resources, while "Rupture" weaves theological understandings into a sustained personal narrative. Our hope is that through this method of doing theology, our readers will come to some insights of their own about what God is saying and doing in their lives and how their own faith traditions can be a resource in their times of sorrow and grief.

One final introductory comment—the title of this book is taken from a verse in the book of Proverbs, "Hope deferred makes the heart sick" (13:12). Infertility is an anguished cycle of hopes raised and hopes dashed; miscarriage and stillbirth are hopes ended. In each form of reproductive loss, hope is focused on a particular pregnancy, a particular dream-child. And in all, hope too soon becomes a cruel source of pain. It does indeed make the heart sick. But hope deferred is not hope extinguished. As Christians we believe that hope triumphs—just how this happens is gracious mystery and the abiding concern of this work.

THE SITTING TIME

Joe Digman, 1981

Don't listen to the foolish unbelievers
    who say forget.
Take up your armful of roses and
    remember them
      the flower and the fragrance.
When you go home to do your sitting
    in the corner by the clock
    and sip your rosethorn tea
It will warm your face and fingers
    and burn the bottom of your belly.
But as her gone-ness piles in white,
    crystal drifts,
It will be the blossom of her moment
    the warmth on your belly,
    the tiny fingers unfolding,
    the new face you've always known,
That has changed you.
Take her moment, and hold it
    As every mother does.
    She will always be
    your daughter
And when the sitting is done you'll find
    bitter grief could never poison
    the sweetness of her time.

ONE *why?*

NADINE PENCE FRANTZ

Two years after we married, we stopped using birth control and eagerly awaited the time I would be pregnant. Each month that I continued to menstruate was a blow, but we would pick ourselves up, listen to statistics about how long it took the average couple to get pregnant, and keep waiting with high hopes. After a year of trying we went to our family physician and were reassured; after two years we went to a fertility specialist. After six years, the accumulated months of failure had taken their toll, and we needed to stop all temperature monitoring, medical pills and injections, all extractions and inseminations, and just cry.

It was painful and unfair. It was not how it was supposed to happen. It wasn't as we had been promised. We were married, we were highly educated, and we had a steady income and large extended families that were ready to receive more grandchildren. We were ready to give of our time and our hearts to a child, and we were given nothing in return, only month after month of bleeding, the sure mark that nothing in my body had changed. It all seemed so arbitrary and unfair. We didn't deserve this, yet this was where we were. We had done everything we were told. We didn't drink or smoke or take in high amounts of caffeine; we didn't engage in high-risk behavior, yet no child was given. We were left exhausted and sexually numb, unable to understand what was happening to us or why.

We grieved, moved forward, and became parents through adoption. We brought a baby boy home from the hospital when he was three days old, and I came to a tender truce with myself about not being able to conceive: "Some women don't do windows, I don't do babies," I would say to myself. But I could be a mom, and so at thirty-two, that part of the promise was fulfilled. We grieved not having a child of our flesh and blood, a mixture of us, but we celebrated having a child to nurture and watch grow.

Thus it was with absolute surprise, ten years later, that I discovered I was pregnant. We hadn't protected against pregnancy for over seventeen years; but in seventeen years, my body had not once nurtured a child. Yet my period was late, I was responding differently to familiar smells, and I felt odd. I didn't even tell my husband when I went at lunchtime to buy a drugstore pregnancy test. It seemed so foolish to even be considering pregnancy, but the test turned positive, and I immediately began reading the literature to see what could cause a false positive. Breathing a familiar sigh of resignation, I discovered that a positive result could also come from an ovarian cyst.

Two days later, that is what I emphasized to the young ultra-sound technician when she was checking my abdomen. All of nineteen, confident in her technology and its ability to know, she looked at me with amusement and asked, "You don't think you're pregnant?" "No," I said. "Given my history, it's probably an ovarian cyst from all the infertility drugs that I took. You see, I don't do babies; some women don't do windows, I don't do babies. I have wanted to, all my life, but it's just not what I do. So please check my ovaries and make sure that they are normal."

Ignoring those instructions, she calmly rolled the ultrasound over my belly and pointed to the screen. "See that? That's your uterus. And there, that peanut-shaped thing is the fetus. See that speck of light flashing outside its body? That's its heart beating. Let's measure it; looks like you are six weeks, five days along. You're definitely pregnant."

My world spun. How could this be? My husband and I were both teaching full-time, our son was ten years old. It was a relief to have him finally out of childhood and into the middle school years. We lived in a three-bedroom house—two bedrooms and a study. We felt good being a family of three. A baby? Diapers? Calling babysitter after babysitter to have time to work? Due in October? How does one give birth in October and have a sabbatical at the same time? This wasn't possible and perhaps not even desired anymore. Yet how could we say no to this child that we had always wanted? After tests, after sleepless nights, after canceling my sabbatical plans and fighting for maternity leave, we grew to want this child, to feel ready for it, to anticipate how it would enter our life and change it. That spring I continued with my teaching and lecturing, preparing myself for a fall birth of a baby boy.

But in May, the morning after Mother's Day, I awoke to find that my water had broken and that the baby's umbilical cord was exposed. With a sinking heart, I knew that no fetus could continue in the womb this way and that at twenty weeks, he was too undeveloped to survive outside the womb. It took a full twenty-four hours for my body to give him up, but on May 14, 1996, Jacob Cézanne Frantz was miscarried in the second trimester and my heart was broken, again. We were given an unofficial certificate with imprints of his feet, the blankets that would have been used to wrap him, and sent home to mourn.

QUESTIONING GOD

How could this happen? How could God be so cruel to promise and then take away? Why couldn't I have children like other women? Where is God in all this? What is wrong with me? What purpose does any of this have? Why did this have to happen? What good could come of it? My life was filled with such questions, questions about which I felt deeply, both because I was in the midst of profound grief and brokenness and because I was a theologian and pastor, a person who was supposed to know the answers to such dilemmas of life. Just what kind of God was it that I believed in? Who was it that I preached and taught about? What kind of affirmations about God and life was I prepared to make?[1]

I was teaching a Christology class the spring semester that we lost Jacob. I missed a week of classes and then went back. Sitting tenderly on a stool in front of my class, I shared with them what had happened. I told them of my grief and confessed, "Although we can continue to work together to understand who Jesus is as the Christ, do not ask me how to understand God's providence and care. Those are questions that I cannot answer at this time." My most honest statement in light of my experiences would have been that God was cruel and uncaring.

Our traditional theological assumptions about God's providence and care, especially for those of us who live out our faith in the North American context, center around affirmations of a God who is an active agent in our life and who watches out for each one of us, "counting the hairs on our heads." We assume that God not only holds us in care, but that God's knowledge of our future historical existence is complete. When tragedy comes our way, we are often consoled by arguments that take a variety of three forms: (1) that God has a plan for our lives, which transcends what we know; (2) that suffering and death are means for training or testing in this life; and (3) that in following the path of Christ, suffering and death are meaningful sacrifices and not in vain.

Death of any kind challenges these theological assertions, and as assurances they are especially inadequate when speaking to the loss and pain that accompanies couples when they face into the broken promises of infertility, miscarriage, and stillbirth. To be told that God knows best is to be told that God doesn't want you to have children. To be told that God is doing this to test you is to say that God is a sadist who will use the death of anyone, even a child, to teach you a lesson. To say that it is a meaningful sacrifice is to say that there was something in this particular death that was necessary for God's work to be done. Those reasons do more to question the kind of God we affirm than they do to assure anyone of God's care during deep loss. After experiencing both infertility and miscarriage, I find I must look closer at all three of these theological assertions to see what is at the heart of each.

God Has a Plan

The most common reassurance given to bereaved parents is to say that God has a plan for our lives that transcends what we can know ourselves. The intent in this is to affirm that God is sovereign both in our daily lives and in the promised future. Articulated most vividly within the work of John Calvin (1509–64), God the Creator is the foundational assertion of our being and our lives.[2] God is Creator; we are creatures. This has implications about whether we can ever fully know God's will or God's purpose (we can't) and about whether we can ever fully see or understand our small part in those greater purposes (no).

Asserting that all is in God's hands and that all will be well in some future time is both a promise that the larger purpose of God is good and that our lives must be seen in light of those larger, not always knowable, purposes.

Yet in experiences of infertility, miscarriage, and stillbirth, men and women are not comforted by being told that God has a bigger plan that they will someday understand, nor are they satisfied with the answer that all will work out in the end. These answers discount their prior understandings of God's promise for a future with a family and children and discount their confidence in God's ability to provide for that promise. The assurances portray a God who has everything administratively under control, yet what kind of a God is it who would encourage the desire to have children, nurturing that desire through extended family, church, and community, then deny it or frustrate it at the end? Or, worse, what kind of a God is it who knows all along that this couple would have to subordinate that desire to some other will or plan, yet still encourages its nurture and development? Does this mean that they hadn't been listening to "God's plan" earlier? That the promise itself was misguided or wrong?

We need to come to a different understanding of how God relates to us, as Creator to creatures, and to a different understanding of God's sovereign power. Maybe being a powerful God does not mean being a powerful administrator who has everything under control. Maybe providing for us does not mean having a blueprint or plan for our lives. Maybe the struggle with death is an ongoing struggle in which God is also a participant, rather than a distant onlooker.

This is not to say that we will be able to fully understand how our human lives fit into the larger framework of God's activity and promise. But it is to say that the explanation of God's role as Creator should not trump every human reality as if that reality does not count. What so often happens in the "God knows best" consolation is that we too quickly ask those who grieve and suffer to sublimate the grief and count it as "not real." Loss and despair somehow become incidental to the God who we claim cares for all. It is as if we are comfortable saying that God cares for all in the ideal, but not in the messiness of real life. As if we are saying that God cares for all at a distance, but does not want to be bothered with the nitty-gritty of everyday life in which we dwell. The world is somehow "beneath" God. The fact that this sounds like the twentieth-century North American role of a "good father" should bother us deeply. Have we modeled our image of a caring God on the image of the "caring father" that developed in a growing industrial society that required men to leave home to "care for their families"?

The image of God as the benevolent, providing father who faithfully supports all from a distance to achieve their promised destiny is untenable to people whose deepest, God-given desires and wants are being snatched away by death or by what seems like an arbitrary fate. Honest theological reflection must honor the depth of the promise and the promise-breaking that is experienced by these couples and the resultant pain and loss that they face. If we are going to insist that parents-to-be take comfort in the wider plans of God, then we must be prepared to explain how this particular death, of one who never had a life, plays a role in God's wider plan and how the loss of this particular future for these parents plays a role in God's future.

When talking with a well-meaning friend who was attempting to comfort us with the reassurance that God was still the all-providing, all-wise father, I found myself blurting out, "Well, if that's the case, then he is an incompetent one!" Incompetent or uncaring, either way, the God who is distant and wants us to believe that everything is under control is not up to the task of comforting those who mourn. That God is better staying away from home until the mess is cleaned up.

Death as a Test

Some would comfort the grieving with words that do not appeal to the future but speak of death as training or as a test in the present for the parents' faith. The intent behind this assertion is to affirm that much happens in this life that is hard and painful, yet from which we learn and grow. Its theological foundation is the affirmation that death does not have the final victory and, if we have faith, we will come to see God "face to face" and triumph over those hardships that we have known. Often, this theological view understands "our earthly life" as mostly a "time of trials" or a "vale of tears" that we bear as best we can, learning about God and God's faithfulness as we endure.

Sometimes the enduring of hardships does require that we look beyond to the time when it will be over or things will be better, with the hope that we will gain strength by going through such pain and brokenness. This attitude of endurance through faith is based on the trust that God can and does use even the worst of circumstances to bring about good and justice. But that is a hope that is based in how God can transform even the worst of circumstances, not a declaration that God necessitated such circumstances to happen in order for certain lessons or understandings to take hold.[3]

When we comfort grieving parents with the assertion that they are to learn from this, we assign their desires for the delights of love, relationships, and parenting to the unimportant and inconsequential, as if those delights are trivial to the wider purposes of God. In so doing, we discount the goodness of earthly life and its possible role in God's creative redemption. It is as if we would be better if we hold ourselves back from desiring such delights and loves and if we would live our lives as if none of this matters, or that it matters only in the development of our interior state ("our soul"). According to this, the cosmos is fallen and to be with God we must not place our hope in the things of this world, but learn from its trials and tribulations for the greater life ahead.

The metaphor suggested behind this view is of a school-mistress who keeps us to the tasks that we hate because they will discipline and improve us for the life ahead. This metaphor of a God who is a disciplinarian is coupled with the language that "it is for our own good." To comfort couples who have experienced reproductive loss by saying "think of what you are learning" is to assert that God would take a life as an object lesson for the parents. This imagines a God who is willing to use any means, including killing a loved one, to insure that we get our lessons right.

This theological justification shifts the focus from the one who died to the one being tested or trained and it drives a wedge between that which is seen to be "of God" and that which is "not worthy" of God's care and attention. Life and relationships themselves become a part of those trivial and unimportant pleasures that we are to regard with only private delight and/or shame. It indicts us if we show too much grief for the baby we lost or for the family we wished to enjoy. And we begin to raise basic questions: What does it say about who we are if we value love and life? What is life for if babies can be lost without mourning? If reproductive loss is just another means for testing our own faith, is living itself basically expendable?

The theological questions that it raises are just as troubling. What kind of God do we affirm if we imagine that God would set things up so that our coming to perfection is dependent on the death of another human being? What kind of God do we affirm if we imagine that God is so spiteful toward life itself? How can we reconcile this God with the "God who so loved the world" that God became incarnate, in the flesh, and dwelt among us so that we might know God's grace and glory?

Facing into death in the midst of God's promise is much harder than quickly brushing aside the death and superficially proclaiming that life as one that God did not want. Death and loss through infertility, miscarriage, and stillbirth fundamentally disrupt our easy arguments about God and life. To ignore this disruption is to push aside the stark reality of death that millions of people experience and to ignore aspects of death that people face no matter what the cause.

A Sacrifice

The final theological response is one that is based on the acknowledgment of the suffering and death of Christ and how that functions as an example for our own life and death. This involves accepting one's own suffering or burden as parallel to that which Christ had to bear, and thus it becomes a way that one is bearing one's own cross. This is intended to point to the victory proclaimed by Christians in Christ's resurrection, where it was Christ's sacrifice that enabled the love of God to be known.

But it is problematic in addressing the death of children, infants, or those not yet born, and in addressing the parents who face into these deaths. In referring to the sacrifice of Jesus as the Christ, we are using the model of an adult who acted within a range of decisions that affected the circumstances of his own death. And although it is debated as to how much Jesus chose his death and how much it was forced upon him by either the bent will of humanity or the divine necessity of God, it is not generally debated that his life had a wider intent and meaning than does each of ours or our children's.

Death as a sacrifice for others makes use of a paradigm of redemption that does not fit death in all circumstances. The unspoken assumption is that somebody is better for this death. And this assumption is hard to maintain in the face of death through stillbirth or miscarriage. Who has gained by this death? Who is "better" because this one died? How are we, as parents, aunts, uncles, good friends, better because we have had to sacrifice our hopes of knowing a new young life?

The paradigm of sacrifice for others works when there is a life well lived and a series of life choices made. In reproductive loss, that cannot be said for either the lost life or for the parents. This loss was not a chosen or intentional decision. It is something that had broken in on them, cut across their choices and desires, devastated their hopes and dreams for the future. It is death, it is loss, it is being bereft of the future for which one had hoped. It is a broken promise, not an event that can easily, somehow, be caught up into the sweep of the wider promises of God. Death still has its sting, very deeply, in the death of a hoped-for child.

MOURNING

In infertility, you must mourn the loss of the children you could never have, that particular mix of genes, laughter, and walk that will never come into being, that will never be known. It is the promise of children, God's promise of children, that is swept away from you. You find that your hope is slowly and inexorably gone, dissipated through the many examinations, tests, and old formulas that are listened to and followed with no success. It is waking up one morning and realizing that while others would have you keep on trying—since the doctors always have one more thing to try—your hopes are dead. Facing into infertility is facing into a future that seems to be a void since it is without the children and family for which one had hoped.

In miscarriage, death is not intangible but present with all its accompanying substance and physical pain. When you miscarry, you are faced with blood, with cramps, with uterine matter, and frequently with an identifiable fetus. Your body has expelled something; you may have had a birthlike experience, but the experience was not accompanied by a baby's cry or breath or laughter. Physical matter might be there, but life is not. Those who miscarry mourn the loss of that expected life which was never able to fully come to be, never able to fully draw its first breath. They mourn the death of that which almost was, but now is inexorably gone. Life and its hopes have been snatched away.

At the center of reproductive loss is death. And it is a death that does not fit nicely within the theological and sociological structures that are a part of North American religious life. Our culture resists death and its necessity, and puts huge amounts of our medical resources into fighting it off. Efforts to sustain life are valiant, but we often take them to the extreme, demonstrating our own unease with this limit on our lives and our own inability to accept life on its own terms. We want to set the terms; we want to avoid death at all costs. Or, if we admit that wish is impossible, we want to at least set the time of our death and those of our loved ones. We want to be ready, we want to have lived a full and good life, we want to be finished with our goals and purpose and to have done something that will be remembered by later generations.

We accept death more willingly when it comes after a well-lived life. Then death is not an interruption nor did it cut short someone's time with us. We are able to see the purpose and productivity that was part of someone's life and assess that the person's life was worth living. But when purpose and productivity are not a part of someone's life, we judge that the life has "been wasted."

Reproductive loss brushes aside all the weights and measures of a life that has or has not been productive or well lived. Facing into these losses and deaths forces one to face into sheer loss of a desired, hoped-for, promised-to-be, human being. It is death itself that confounds us; it is the not-being that confronts us, not the sense that this person's purpose in life had been left unfulfilled. Death through miscarriage and stillbirth ends the possibility of human life. It is as simple and as devastating as that.

Encouraging people who are facing the death of a loved one to transcend their situation in order to see the larger good denies the very nature of grief itself. Perhaps others can do it for us, but generally when we are in the midst of despair, mourning, and loss, part of what we have lost is the ability to transcend our situation. We have become this mourning, grieving creature, and the depths of despair do not give us room to detach ourselves from that reality. We collapse into weeping and no longer have emotions, but are our emotions.[4] Many accounts of grieving tell of the loss of the sense of self and of the future. Who we are has been irreparably changed by this death. We have lost a baby that we wanted and loved, and we are now lost as well.

Because of the relational nature of self and identity, the living must remake themselves after a death. This is the crux of the grief work; death shatters the present self, and the question becomes "who am I, now?" with this death, with this loss of a future? Falling into grief, the familiar self and its constructs disappear, which is when we sense the utter absence of God and the need for complete reconstruction.[5] One cannot just step outside of that breaking apart and reconstructive work by transcending it or quickly "getting over it." The only consolation that can be imagined in the moment of grief is having the baby in one's arms. And that is now impossible.

PROMISE

"Blessed are the poor in spirit, for theirs is the kingdom of heaven. Blessed are those who mourn, for they will be comforted" (Matt. 5:3–4). In the midst of his Sermon on the Mount, Jesus of Nazareth spoke these words. Enigmatic and the focus of much study, these words remembered through centuries of Christian faith affirm that life is worthy of mourning, that life is full of God-givenness, and that when loss and death occurs—the tearing of the soul from the one who has been loved—it is worthy of grief, mourning, and the rending of garments.[6]

Each and every death, no matter how it has occurred, ends a particular life. Maybe this is too obvious to say. Death ends that wonderfully random and miraculous set of characteristics that came together to be that person who stood before you, who laughed beside you, who played around you, or whom you hoped would be your child. Death cuts short the delight that could have been known, the future that almost was. Death ends a particular life and a particular future. This is why we must stop and mourn. Yet we know that although death may not always be understandable, death is not outside the life of God.

That is what we learn when we mourn. Mourning cuts to the heart of the matter as it cuts to the heart of the person. Mourning, through its recognition of loss, sees clearly. It sees that it is the delight of being with this particular one who has been lost. It sees that being with people, being with God, living in the midst of this wonderful, crazy, blooming world is what life is about. Life is God's, all of it. And we are foolish to think that we can assign a purpose or a message to death, as if we are at life's center. Life is God's. God created life and God delights in its very being. And even those who are lost to us before their time are somehow still in the delight of God. Mourning their loss, mourning our loss, is an affirmation of the delight of life that is not fully ours.

Our confidence is based in God, not because God is unaffected by our pain and grief but because God did go through this earthly life with us and does go through it with us now. God has gone through the grief and suffering with the millions who are in the world and have been a part of the world since the beginning. Whatever understanding of God that is offered to grieving parents as hope for the future must be offered in light of the death and loss that they have experienced. Knowing that God is with us is an affirmation that life will go on, that love and relationships will be possible again, even though this anticipated one, this baby, is gone.

God's Incarnational Presence

During my experiences of infertility and miscarriage, the most comfort came when I was able to have the clear sense that God was grieving with me in the loss of the children that I could not bear and in the loss of the future that we desired. In these times, what became profoundly present to me was the active, comforting sense of God being with us in the midst of this tragedy, not of God holding back or staying distant from us until we got better.

This active sense of God's presence is found in a stream of Christian thought that emphasizes the sacramental presence of God in our everyday lives through the activity and presence of the Spirit. Grounded in the incarnational presence of God in the very being of Jesus as the Christ, this model of God coming to us—becoming human with us—reaffirms that the world can be the dwelling place of God. As articulated by theologian Sallie McFague, "the world is our meeting place with God."[7] Instead of seeking to alleviate the grief of couples through minimizing their ties to the hoped-for baby and family life, articulating a sense of God's presence can reassure them that even though this loss has occurred, God is still with them and that God knows their pain.

This requires a theology that insists that God is actively present in earthly matters and delights in our delight. It requires a theology that understands earthly matters—fleshly, concrete, particular matters of birth, death, love, betrayal—as being the heart of what God cares about, not some distant time or place that will be above or beyond all earthly existence. Instead of God being powerful through the ability to keep everything under control and within a prearranged plan, God's power comes from being the vital source that enlivens all of life. This source of vital power blesses the cosmos with constant renewal, grace, and redemption, even as life may sometimes still exemplify death, betrayal, and destruction.[8]

We cannot deny that there is brokenness in this existence or a separation from God that we frequently know and that profoundly affects all that we are and do. But that brokenness and separation is not the final word, and consoling those in the midst of such brokenness requires us to stress God's ability to be present to them, not God's distant waiting for them to buck up and get over it. God is a participant with us in our grief; that is our consolation and how we know God's care.

Death must be faced for what it is—an end to a love and an end to a life to which one was intimately attached either through actual relationship or through hopes and expectations. Life and relationships are what God celebrates and are that in which God delights. To depict God otherwise is to do great injustice to the scriptural witness and the witness of the vitality of God's spirit. Earthly life has a role in God's creative redemption. We are not asked to hold ourselves back from desiring delight and love. And when death removes a life from among us, we feel the loss and the void. It is the role of the faith community and the larger traditions of the Christian community (such as the ongoing liturgy and witness of the faith) to sustain the promise and hope when those in mourning cannot for themselves. As the living remake themselves, as they gather their fragmented souls from the shattering nature of death, the faith community carries them into a future that they cannot see or even conceptualize at the time of their mourning.

To speak of the promise of the future, one must speak of the promise of life and loves and relationships that God can still make possible. The hope that is offered is one of a future that will somehow also contain delight even though this anticipated life ended in death and despair. The promise that is given through the graceful redemption of God is that life can still be blessed, even though death has occurred. The promise that continues is that God's spirit can still move among us, even though we are collapsed into the deepest grief that we have ever known.

Blessed are we who mourn, for by mourning we acknowledge both our deepest desires for life and our deepest brokenness in light of death. Blessed are we who mourn, for we will know the realm of God where all such desires are known and held in comfort and care. Blessed are we who mourn, for God will be with us as we grieve.

For as I take up my armful of roses, I remember the Jacob we lost and who changed me. As I take his moment and hold it, he will always be my son. "And when the sitting is done you'll find bitter grief could never poison the sweetness of [his] time." So be it.

OTWOCK VII

Kadya Molodowsky, ca. 1923–24

Good health to you! My women friends
Already have babies in white cradles
And bend tenderly over them
With quiet, motherly faces,
With full, naked breasts—
The girl's life is gone.

And they look quietly over to me,
With damp luster and dark gazes,
Like the black look of water in autumn
On the eve of freezing over.

For them, the days don't end
With exuberant evenings
Or with long strolls in the streets,
Their lips wearing a desolate smile,
As it happens to me.

Sleeping quietly, their round faces
On full-bellied, white pillows,
They stretch out a sleepy hand to the cradle.

And they don't, in the twilight of dawn
Send pale glances
To the gray windowpane
For someone's unfinished word
Or for someone's smile

Repeating itself on my lips.

My women friends already have babies

In white cradles.

Good health to you!

—Translated from the Yiddish
by Kathryn Hellerstein

TWO *sorrow*

MARY T. STIMMING

M ass on Mother's Day. During the five years that my husband and I struggled with infertility, we repeatedly debated whether to attend services on that Sunday. Familiar with the traditional Mother's Day rituals at our parish, we usually declined to go. It had become too painful to watch others collect their flowers and stand for applause. Even now, an adoptive mother of four, I go reluctantly, with trepidation. Unable to give birth, I know that I am not the type of mother called to mind on this secular feast day.[1]

33

I know too that this day is not one easily entered by those who have miscarried or endured a stillbirth. Our longings, our tears, our despair on this day are discomforting to others and ourselves. Were we to plan a portion of the liturgy I wonder what readings we might choose. The desperate cries of Sarah, Rachel, and Hannah for children are our own. Yet, each of their stories ends in pregnancy and childbirth, and there I part ways. I know there is deeper theological meaning in these Barren Matriarch narratives, but on Mother's Day I search for a story of someone whose desires went unfulfilled.[2] Maybe it is the story in the Gospels of the woman with the hemorrhage (Mark 5:25–34). I know her. I know what it is to have blood flow without stop, to have it drain you and mock you, to have it set you outside the circle of your friends.

DESIRE

From earliest childhood, I wanted to be a mother. I remember playing pregnancy with a small pillow tucked under my shirt. If memory serves, I did this again the one time the clinic called with a positive pregnancy test. I labeled a small bottle of champagne "Dad" and a small bottle of milk "Mom" and waited, with my pillow, to share the long-awaited news with my husband. But, within days, the hormone levels plummeted and I never was, nor pretended to be, pregnant again.

Sometimes it is hard for me to recall how much I once wanted to be pregnant, how much I went through in an ultimately futile quest to have a baby. The intensity of desire for a child through pregnancy and birth is well known and well documented. It is certainly a biologically sensible drive and one that has enjoyed a certain measure of theological approval. Although desire usually receives a cool reception in religious circles, some thinkers have found in it a window into the believer's relationship with God. Ignatius of Loyola (1491–1556) counseled his followers to seek God in their desires. The process of discernment he elaborated to determine whether a desire led to or away from God is complex, but its conviction that desires can be ways we relate to God and God to us is instructive. Desire for children per se is not theologically problematic. What is problematic is inordinate desire, and early in the infertility ordeal I passed into this realm. The desire for pregnancy became all-consuming. Time, money, physical and emotional resources were all devoted to and depleted by the rigors of the infertility regimen.[3] I have heard—and believe—that infertility patients are second only to terminally ill cancer patients in their willingness to endure treatments with even the slightest glimmer of hope. Even as I descended into an obsession with getting pregnant, I was haunted by Paul Tillich's *Dynamics of Faith*, a slender volume I had read in college. In the opening chapter, Tillich describes faith as holding something as one's "ultimate concern." What this something is varies. According to Tillich, one's ultimate concern has two hallmarks: it makes an "unconditional demand" that everything be sacrificed for its sake and it promises that its attainment will deliver "ultimate fulfillment." One example he provides is success. Someone whose ultimate concern is success is prepared to sacrifice all for its sake (health, home, principles) in the expectation that it will produce complete fulfillment.[4]

Biological parenthood and the pursuit of pregnancy towards this end can, I'm convinced, become one's ultimate concern. It was mine. It became the center of my life. From my conversations in infertility support groups and clinic waiting rooms, I don't think I'm the only one. In fact, for others, it took on an even darker ultimacy. I listened as women sacrificed marriages and long-held moral principles for the sake of pregnancy and biological parenthood. Each of us told ourselves "once I get pregnant everything will be perfect," "once I have a baby everything will be perfect." And then either that didn't happen and we were devastated —that which promised ultimate fulfillment failed to deliver—or it did and those women still didn't feel ultimately fulfilled on every level at every moment.

The harsh truth hit home. Pregnancy and biological parenthood are not the ultimate realities. Promises were made that could not be sustained. They are not worth the renunciation of all else; they cannot offer endless and complete fulfillment. In Tillichian categories, pregnancy and biological parenthood can become a form of false faith, an instance of idolatry. By "idolatry," Tillich does not mean worshipping statues or golden calves. Rather, idolatry is placing one's faith in that which is not truly ultimate.

Idolatry does not occur in a vacuum. In the case of pregnancy and biological parenthood, social expectations are powerful amplifiers of personal desires. In *Family Bonds: Adoption and the Politics of Parenthood,* Elizabeth Barthelot documents the existence of a strongly pronatalist culture, one that nearly worships biological parenthood, in contemporary America. Comparing the social benefits offered to biological versus adoptive parents, she finds repeated favoritism of the former. Our employers offer extensive financial coverage of the costs of infertility treatment, pregnancy, and birth; they offer little or none for adoption. Employers offer automatic maternity leaves (under the heading of disability!) for women who give birth; they force women who adopt to rewrite policies if they want equal time off. The law makes hallow and nearly inviolable the rights of biological parents; it presents risk to the permanency of adoption.[5] Many infertile women describe their experience as one of "not being a real woman," "being on the outside looking in." The extent to which they feel inadequate, like outsiders, is in part a measure of the weight our culture has put on motherhood.

ENVY

The identification of essential femaleness with mothering no doubt contributes to the pervasiveness of envy among the infertile. Although not a universal response to infertility, envy is common. Two writers recall the bond they forged as "we could divulge the feelings of displaced anger and jealousy we harbored over a friend who was pregnant, a cousin who had popped out baby number two."[6] Their honesty no doubt prompts sad nods of recognition among their readers. During the years my husband and I struggled with infertility, every trip to our local suburban mall brought my envy and resentment to the surface. The throngs of pregnant women and the mothers pushing strollers brought out the worst in me.

Envy receives relatively little attention in contemporary psychological literature. More research and analysis is devoted to its sister experience, jealousy. As in the quotation above, it is common in casual speech to use the terms "envy" and "jealousy" interchangeably and, according to some definitions, there is some overlap between the two. But in general, philosophy, theology, and psychology recognize important distinctions between them. Broadly speaking, the defining feature of jealousy is the "sense of right . . . to the exclusive possession of a thing."[7] In contrast, envy does not claim sole proprietorship over a good. The envious do not dispute the rights of others to some good, but they insist on their fair share; or even a little more if they perceive themselves as more deserving.[8] Bearing these definitions in mind, I find envy, not jealousy, more accurately characterizes many infertile persons' stance towards the fertile world.

There is a long tradition of philosophical and theological reflection on envy. Unfortunately, only one aspect of this rich line of thought ever reaches most of us—the inclusion of envy among the seven deadly sins. But according to such thinkers as Aristotle (384–322 B.C.E.) and Thomas Aquinas (ca. 1225–74), envy is a more complex phenomenon. Reflecting on my experience in light of these complexities has both comforted and chastened me. Although all the psychology texts I consulted on infertility assured me that envy was to be expected, this response struck me as inadequate. Self-help literature abounded in suggestions on how, graciously, to minimize such contact and how to accept the eruption of such powerful reactions within oneself: send a gift to a friend's baby shower instead of attending, go late and leave early from the family holiday gathering. Was it proverbial Catholic guilt that prevented me from being satisfied with such counsel?

My dissatisfaction prompted me to reread Thomas on envy.[9] Thomas opens his consideration of envy with the question, "Whether envy is a form of sorrow?" Simply reading this moved me to tears as it captures the essence of envy that had eluded me. I had long been aware of envy's poisoned edge, but the grief at its core was obscure until I read Thomas's formulation.

Thomas proposes that the sorrow that is envy "may come about in four ways." First, he observes, we may grieve for another's good "through fear that it may cause harm" either to oneself or one's goods. Second, we may "grieve over another's good, not because he has it, but because the good which he has, we have not." Third, we may grieve because we judge the one possessing the good to be unworthy of it. And fourth, we may grieve over another's good in so far as that "good surpasses ours." For Thomas, only this fourth type is "true envy." The first he classifies as "fear"; the second, in some circumstances, as "zeal"; and the third as "indignation."

Initially, the third form of envy jumped out as most applicable to me, that is, the sorrow over another's good occasioned by our judgment that the one possessing it is unworthy of it. In this circumstance, it is both the good desired and the perceived unworthiness of the possessor that combine to produce "indignation." Thomas has in mind temporal goods, such as wealth, that can belong to anyone regardless of moral status. While Thomas thought of money, I thought of pregnancy. How it drove me mad to see the too young, too immature, too mean, too something glowing Madonnas. I didn't know what bothered me more: that they were *pregnant* and I was not or that *they* were pregnant. I thought to myself, "I'd make a better mother than that fifteen-year-old, that disinterested lady, that short-tempered, sharp-tongued ogre in the check-out line." To my surprise, Thomas acknowledges that some are undeserving of the goods they possess. But there is, Thomas warns, a distrust of God's providence involved in indignation. We don't know how God is working through a particular good in another's life. Moreover, indignation blinds us to higher, more valuable goods.

Over time, I returned to Thomas's analysis of the second type of sorrow as the one closest to my experience. In this type of envy, we "grieve over another's good, not because he has it, but because the good which he has, we have not." More than anything it was my lack of pregnancy that fueled my envy—not the relative virtue of pregnant friends and strangers, not their fertility, but my infertility. The distinction is an important one. As far as I recall, and I admit I may be sweetening my recollections, I did not begrudge others' their pregnancies. I could share in the happiness of their good news. But the happiness was accompanied by torrents of tears over my inability to conceive and carry a child.

Leaving aside the subtleties of the ensuing analysis, Thomas concludes that such sorrow, such envious sorrow, is definitely lamentable and possibly spiritually dangerous. This type of envy is usually experienced in a rush, a surge. It is a fusion of volition and emotion. We exist in a therapeutic culture that lulls us with the refrain that "feelings aren't good or bad, they're just feelings." We are told that only our actions are subject to moral evaluation, not our feelings. But there are situations in which some responses seem more right than others. To delight in good health and to be distressed over an injured animal seem right; delight over an injured animal and distress over good health seem wrong. So there is something about how we feel that belongs to the moral realm. Thomas theorizes that this is because how we feel about things,

what passions we exhibit, reveals who we are, what habits of character we've cultivated. Thus, envy that is largely the result of emotions can rightly be considered objectionable because it indicates
that a breeding ground for such a passion has been cultivated
within you, by you.[10] Still, Thomas holds, the problem is not so
much with envy in itself, but that it is an easy gateway for more
corrupting processes.

The most serious form of envy according to Thomas is that
which is opposed to "charity." The hallmark of this type of envy is
that it leads us to resent and not to rejoice over our neighbor's
good. It is no longer sorrow over one's lack thereof, but the bitter
resentment of another's possession of the desired good. And this,
for Thomas, is spiritual death ("mortal sin") because it refuses to
love a good that belongs to another. In this refusal, we are alien-
ated from the ultimate good and the source of all good, God.

I never thought much about what envy does to its object until
a friend who lost a baby late in the second trimester of her pregnancy told me what it was like to be the recipient of envious
glances. She said that when the baby was living it made her feel
guilty over her good fortune; after the baby died, it made her
angry that others were presumptuous about the true state of her
being. She was living with a dead child inside and others assumed
she was smug and flaunting. I think too of a friend who conceived
through treatment and the lonely, anxious path she trod, or the
friends whose ambivalence about their impending motherhood
shadowed their experience of pregnancy. When I indulged my
envy of pregnant women, I was not open to the possibility that
they were in need of comfort too. My imagination stunted, I re-
duced them to a single reality—that which I sought and desired so
deeply. This envy damages and may sever the bonds between us.

If Karl Rahner is correct that love of God and love of neighbor are two sides to one coin, then we see what Thomas means by
envy as an affront to charity, an affront to God.[11] Invoking the

term "sin" in this context is theologically appropriate but pastorally delicate. As Thomas demonstrates, not every reaction we label as envy truly merits the term. Moreover, in the instances that do, not every episode of envy is equally problematic, let alone morally or spiritually culpable. The envy that springs from deep pain, from yearnings denied, requires sensitive treatment. For myself, recognizing the sinful dimensions of such envy did not make me feel worse, but better. It prompted me to turn to God for healing and it opened my eyes to the larger forces distorting my views of self and others.

HOPE

For me the gracious word that restored my hope was a saying of my grandfather's: "You are a child of God and that alone is sufficient." Grampy was one of the world's rare individuals who could say this without sounding sanctimonious or preachy. The sincerity with which he held this belief shone through in his dealings with everyone he encountered. From the janitor in his office to the mayor of our city, he treated everyone as embodiments of divine love. Infertility blinded me to this truth. The truth didn't disappear but it was elusive. One woman who became pregnant after years of struggling to conceive commented, "For the first time in my life I not only *knew* God loved me; I *felt* it." After she miscarried at ten weeks she "did not feel abandoned by God . . . but the feeling of being abundantly loved was gone."[12] Hope is reborn when this sense of being abundantly loved is rekindled.

Although much in the Christian tradition reinforces and perpetuates the equation of women with their childbearing, strands do exist that broaden our sense of self. The encyclical *Mulieris Dignitatem*, for example, took tremendous heat in feminist circles for its narrow conception of women.[13] According to it, all women are mothers of a sort; women in religious life are "spiritual mothers," and so on. And it credits women with stronger spiritual capacity for love owing to our biological capacity for pregnancy. However, within the same text lurk passages of promise. It speaks of women's full share in *imago dei* and their call to discipleship in baptism. These passages need expansion. They offer "good news" to the infertile. They recognize the theological equality of all as children of God, and the ramifications of this are tremendous.

A theological reminder that we are not defined by our fertility, or lack thereof, is tonic for those of us battered by our own and others' expectations of biological parenthood. We may never bear children. We may never raise children. But that is secondary to our identity as children of God. We cannot allow infertility to rob us of our dignity, our blessedness, and our vocations in the world. Others may pity us and see us as somehow inferior and inadequate. Sometimes we see ourselves that way too; that is when the church must speak the good news to us and assist as we expand our vision of who we are and who we are called to be.

Prior to reproductive loss, we had a vision of who we were and who we would be. Infertility, miscarriage, and stillbirth annul our expectations and force us to re-imagine our future. We must, in the words of poet Wendell Berry, live "the given life, and not the planned."[14] It is difficult to let go of the life we had planned and we grieve the loss of the moments we had happily anticipated. The recognition that I would never feel a child move within me or nurse a newborn brought tremendous sadness. What I had deeply desired, what I had envied in others, was not going to be.

In some respects, the tears and tantrums that accompanied letting go of the "planned" life were easier than accepting the "given." Numerous rituals, religious and secular, presented themselves as ways to enact the death of my husband's and my dreams of biological parenthood. In the end, we settled on casting shells back into the ocean with a prayer. The shells represented the biological children we had hoped for and would never have, and the ocean symbolized God, the matrix of life from whom we come and to whom we return. I don't recall the words of our prayer, but we asked for peace and the strength to chart a new course in our lives together.

I suspect that part of what makes charting this new course so painful for those experiencing reproductive loss is that it requires us to hope again. For most of us, by the time we are metaphorically or literally burying the children we longed for, hope has become the enemy, something we fight against to protect ourselves from more disappointment and despair. I remember that early in our years of infertility I thought with fondness of a statue I had seen in Spain during college. It was a carved image of the Virgin Mary large with child. Perhaps it was not the first pregnant Madonna statue I had seen, but for some reason it is the most memorable. Her title, "Madonna Esperanza," Our Lady of Hope, confirmed my confidence that it was right and good for me to want a baby and that in time I too would be a Mary on her way to Bethlehem. As months passed and no child grew in my womb, my memory of this statue became bittersweet. Her title seemed to mock me.

But in the later years of our infertility, as we began to explore the possibility of adoption, the theological truth of that statue finally came to me. It was a truth any reasonably attentive Sunday school child might have known but the fog of grief around infertility had left me blind. This was Our Lady of Hope not because she was pregnant, but because she is *Theotokos*, the God-bearer. The pregnant Madonna is a symbol of Christian hope because she embodies the reality of Emmanuel, God-with-us. Her gift is not bearing a child but bearing the Christ child and this, Christians profess, is promised to us all.

Of course, bearing Christ within us means that the rhythm of death and resurrection will pervade our lives. Some infertile women describe their unwanted menstruations as a monthly descent into death. For the woman longing for pregnancy, blood becomes tangible proof of the absence of life. This experience of blood stands in tension with biblical language that regards blood as the essence of life. Even attempts to subsume this flow of blood into Christ's outpouring in the crucifixion falter. The Gospels present Christ's blood as voluntary self-sacrifice, the means of salvation; menstrual blood for the infertile is involuntary and the instrument of torment.

I suspect that my Irish grandmother would counsel, "offer it up," as a way of identifying the suffering my period brought with that of Christ. But this fails to satisfy. It is too general; it ignores the specific loss endured each month. Of more comfort for me is the theology of blood promoted by the theologian-scientist Pierre Teilhard de Chardin. In "The Mass on the World," Chardin speaks of the blood of Christ present in the eucharistic wine as representative of that which is taken from us, that which is, like wine from the grape, pressed out of us. For him the wine, the blood, is the suffering we undergo, not the suffering we undertake. According to this poetic essay, eucharistic wine symbolizes all the "fearful forces of dissolution." Communion with this wine unites our experiences of diminishment with Christ and hence sanctifies them in him.[15]

This theology appeals to me. It does not soften the harsh, often bitter, edges of life. It preserves the involuntary nature of certain forms of suffering. And it acknowledges that such instances diminish us. But, wonderfully, without minimizing their tragedy it finds in these occasions of grief occasions of grace.

Blood and death is not how we would describe our ideal meeting place with God. But it may be where God is found. Not the Santa Claus God who rewards virtue and punishes vice; not the grandparent God who gives us what we want; but the resurrecting God who teaches us to "sing in the shadow of the cross." Our song may not be the one we originally hoped to sing. It may not be the one we practiced. But we can learn a new melody, maybe one with a somber counterpoint, and it can soar.

A FLOWER AND NOT A FLOWER

Po Chu-I, ca. 820–29

A flower and not a flower;

of mist yet not of mist;

At midnight she was there;

she went as daylight shone.

She came and for a little while

was like a dream of spring,

And then,

as morning clouds that vanish traceless,

she was gone.

—Translated from the Chinese
by Duncan Mackintosh

45

THREE *rupture*

Serene Jones

CALL

Come down and sit in the dust,
O virgin daughter of Babylon;
sit on the ground without a throne . . .
ISAIAH 47:1a, RSV

Wendy called me late Saturday afternoon. It was pouring rain when I arrived, and she shivered as she pulled on her raincoat and stumbled into the backyard. Handing me a spoon from her kitchen, she explained what she wanted. We knelt together in a far corner, away from the street. With knees sunk in mud, we began digging.

I did most of the work; she kept slipping sideways and finally just gave up and sat down, crying, seeming not to notice that her hands and face were covered with dirt. When the hole was deep enough, Wendy leaned forward and pulled out of her raincoat pocket an old white handkerchief, crumpled loosely. Her grandmother Idabel's, she told me. Unfolding it carefully as she placed it in the shallow grave, she showed me what I didn't want to see: pieces of tissue, bloody, unrecognizable.

After staring for what seemed like hours, she looked at me for the first time since I'd arrived. "You're the minister, Serene. What should we do now?" she asked.

The time had come, it seemed, for words to be spoken, for something profound and sermonic sounding to be pronounced, or perhaps for verses poetic and sad to flow forth. Something ancient. Music should have started, a faint guitar, a haunting flute, or bagpipes whining out a mournful "Amazing Grace."

But nothing came. No words, no familiar melody. Only silence. My knee slipped and I dropped into the mud beside her.

"I don't know what to say, sweetie."

Rainwater and mud had begun forming murky pools in the dirty cloth. Wendy laid her head on my shoulder and then turned her body into mine. "I want my mommy," she whispered as she grew more fetal. I closed my eyes and wrapped my arms around her.

"Please, God, receive this: our will, broken; our hope, lost; our body, ruptured; our blood, poured out; our womb, a grave."

The words left me before I could catch them. And there was no amen. Just more rain and a long silence. Wendy finally reached out and threw a handful of mud into the hole. "Let's go inside," she said, her voice now growing slightly steadier. Offering my most confident pastoral intervention of the day, I answered back. "I'll make the tea."

We sat together late into the evening, eating soup and drinking wine, the first alcohol Wendy had tasted for almost four months. She had been bleeding for three days and looked ghostly. Fifteen weeks into a long-awaited pregnancy, she had miscarried, an event now marked by the awkward, rain-soaked funeral rite we had just finished.

She had called me to be with her because only six months earlier I had lost, for the second time in a year, a twelve-week pregnancy. At the time, we hadn't known each other well, but a friend had recommended her as a massage therapist who was good at "this sort of thing." During the worst of it, she had come to my house and for hours massaged my legs and rubbed deep into the hollowed flesh beneath my ankle, hoping to ease the flow of death out of my body. "An old wives' tale," she told me as she worked, pausing now and then to light a candle, burn some sage, and put crystals in my hands. My husband had been close by as well, but neither his hands nor his heart had been able to touch me in the knowing ways that she had. "The dashed-dreams Doula," I had jokingly dubbed her several weeks later: midwife of lost hopes.

When Wendy had called me earlier that day, I was surprised to find that now it was my skills she needed. "I want to do something sacred, and I want some minister-type person to do it. I need help. I can't be alone, but I can't bring myself to call Paul in Boston. I would have to take care of him, and right now, I can't do it. I can hardly sit up. And I can't stop crying."

Something sacred? Of course, I had thought. This kind of event screamed for ritual, begged for liturgical recognition. Throughout my own miscarriages, I had wanted and waited for something religious to happen—for a divine presence to enter into the space of my grieving and give me comfort, for the touch of a savior who might open to me the boundless stretch of grace, for the voices of a community that could remind me of life's precious persistence in the midst of such loss.

I had fantasized about a pastor visiting, but no one had come. Of course, I never called my pastor to tell him. It had seemed too private a matter and besides, in the entire thirty-five years of my life in Christian congregations, I had never seen or heard anyone talk theologically about reproductive loss, much less participated in a worship service devoted to it. I recalled as well that during seminary, our pastoral care courses had no sections dealing with the grief associated with infertility, stillbirth, or miscarriage, even though we had long and sensitive discussions of "women's issues" like breast cancer, rape, abortion, and domestic violence.

I had also fantasized about covens of women like my sisters, mother, and grandmother gathering around me and chanting ancient words of solace. But that wasn't to be either. I lived thousands of miles from my mother, and most of the chants I had learned in my local women's worship group began by invoking "God our Mother." Just the thought of these words had filled me with fierce anger. How could I pray to such a maternal God, one who had successfully become a mother when I could not? My beloved feminist rhetoric seemed, in this situation, sardonic and cruel.

And now Wendy was asking me to bring a sense of the sacred to her grief. The idea panicked me, but I had blurted out the inevitable, "Of course. I am coming right over." She probably even expected me to pray.

As I had pulled on my slicker and walked to the car, I remembered the anxiety I had felt during my own miscarriage about what to call, in prayer, the tissue I was losing. I still didn't know. Wendy and I are both strong pro-choice activists and had been horrified at conservative attempts to treat the abortion of an early pregnancy as child murder. So, it didn't seem right, now, for me to pray for a lost life. And yet, the grief that had welled up in me only six months earlier was for a child I had wanted, desperately wanted, but could not have. Language had failed me, then, in ways profound and confusing, and I had no reason to believe that the gift of speech would somehow miraculously come to me, just because Wendy needed it.

So I had arrived on her doorstep burdened by the awful weight of my inadequacy to the task ahead. Yet it was not just my inadequacy, but the church's and feminism's as well. I knew of no prayer books to turn to, no earth-mother chants to invoke, no well-wrought cronish wisdom to ponder, and no time-tested images of God to crawl into. All I arrived with was the promised companionship of a shared grief and a common desire for grace somehow, somewhere, and in some way to touch us here.

LAMENT

Cry aloud, spare not . . .

ISAIAH 58:1a, RSV

It took Wendy an hour to sip down her first bowl of soup that afternoon. She hadn't said much since we'd come inside around four. Mostly she had just sat at the kitchen table, rocking slowly. Standing only a few feet away, I hovered over the stove, stirring. "Do you want more soup?"

"Sure." She pulled the blanket around her tighter. "It's pretty good, isn't it?" A small dash of pride shot across her face. "I started making it right after the bleeding began. Pulled out a chicken and went to chopping vegetables, grinding spices. Threw tons of stuff in, anything I could find: rice, potatoes, carrots, pasta, leftover bean salad. I wanted," she paused and looked out the window, "I wanted to do something I had control over. To create something good and whole."

For the first three hours after my own bleeding had started, I had sat at my office at Yale and furiously graded papers left over from the end of spring term. They were papers on Calvin's view of providence, of all things. The doctor had called around two o'clock to tell me I was "spontaneously aborting." By five, I had a large stack of completed work beside me, work that certified my status as—I could hear my mother's voice saying it quite proudly—"a modern professional woman, capable of achieving whatever she puts her mind to." By six, my focused resolve had started to wear thin, however, and by seven, I was at home, curled up in my bed, not crying, just lying there, as still as I could, trying hard to will the bleeding to stop.

"Please don't do this," I had begged my body. Never in my life had I wanted something as badly as I wanted to be a mother and have a child—or so it felt in the moment. And never had I been so numbingly aware that my will could do nothing to achieve it. "Capable of doing anything I want." What a joke, I'd thought. "I can choose my future," yeah, right. It felt like some weird feminist farce.

In the weeks that followed my miscarriage, I descended into a dark pit of helplessness, a place of despair.[1] Consumed by a feeling of utter powerlessness, I found it hard to do anything, not just have a baby, but anything. Sipping soup, constructing a sentence that began and ended coherently and then speaking it, being a person, they all required more will than I had.

Wendy's voice pulled me back to the present. "I haven't had a cigarette in years. Do you think there's much nicotine left in me? Maybe I shouldn't have had sex last weekend. I don't even like Paul that much. Not enough to risk losing this chance at a child. Damn, how did I mess this up?"

Her words reminded me that stealthily wrapped around despair is its ugly twin sister, guilt. I too was often plagued by the awful suspicion that I could have done something to stop my miscarriages from happening. Desperate to retrieve a sense of power, I had gone over my past, again and again, in my mind, trying to uncover the secret cause of them all: What did I do to make this happen? What did I do? Was it yesterday's shrimp salad? Should I have taken more folic acid? Maybe if my mother had nursed me? Is this what I get for having a career? Did the stress of teaching finally push my body over the edge? Or was it the pressure of the article I had just finished?

In all these varied guises, the specter of culpability appeared before me in all its glory, insisting that at the very moment I felt most powerless, everything was most insistently my fault. That first evening, as I lay in bed trying to will the bleeding to stop, I remember convincing myself that I hadn't drunk enough water to keep my uterus hydrated. That's why I would never have this child. I'd done this awful thing: forgotten to have an extra glass of water with lunch.

"Serene, do you think it's because I had an abortion when I was eighteen?" Wendy asked me. I knew she didn't believe in divine punishment or that her abortion was wrong but at this moment, that didn't matter. Somewhere, deep inside her lurked that oddly empowering desire to lay the blame somewhere in her actions.

I turned down the burner's heat and sat next to her. "No, that's not it."

"Then maybe it was the drugs I did in college. Remember how they told us if we took acid, it would deform our babies." And from there, the list went on. A long accounting of all the sins she had committed or at least thought she had, all those bad decisions and thoughtlessly dangerous actions she wanted to believe had brought her to this point in time. And to me, it wasn't clear which hurt worse: the possibility that she caused it, or that she had absolutely no control over it at all.[2]

God, receive this: our will, broken.

Around six, Wendy's sister's voice leaped out at us from the answering machine. "Hi, missy. I just called to see how things are going. Still got that morning sickness? Listen, when I had it, Mom told me to try that gross stuff they give old people. Ensure, I think. I kept it down, but yuck. Call me when you get a chance."

I had met Laura several weeks before. Her thick black hair and slightly bucked teeth had made it clear she was Wendy's sister, to say nothing of the way they pronounced their "t"s and the almost identical black sweaters they had worn. Would Wendy's baby have the same thick hair and funny sounding speech? It had delighted me to think so. I had found myself imagining a little girl, a very cute one, riding her bicycle between two graying, adoring sisters. "Don't answer it." Wendy told me. "I can't bear to tell her. We were planning a beach vacation this summer, with kids. Her Johnny is two. I could just see him playing with my little one's tiny fingers." Her gaze wandered off somewhere, probably to the seashore her hoped-for child would never see.

From the moment the small pink strip appeared on my pregnancy test, I had begun filling up my future with the story of the child who was coming. I never imagined a general child or a nameless baby. No, it was always a particular child. This one. She'll have my father's nose, I liked to think, or maybe my sister's basketball skills. And the time she filled in my imagined future was not just any time. It was her history, our history. I would take her to India when she turned twelve. On my fifty-fifth birthday, she would come home from college, maybe bringing a special friend. Tears had welled in my eyes when I saw her crying at my funeral. These and many other pictures of the future had filled my thoughts and so overwhelmed my previous plans that this vision of me as mother with my daughter quickly became the most important story in my mental universe. My expectation, my pregnant expecting, became the reflexive content of all my hoping.

So when I had curled up in bed after finishing my grading, I was weighed down not only by my own powerlessness but also the reality of my futurelessness. With the bleeding had come the sense that my body had come unstuck in time. My anchor in history had come unmoored, and I was drifting off into a strangely nontemporal, desolate world.

The answering machine finally clicked off and Wendy started rocking again. "I can't find words," she said.

"I know. I know." It was the only answer I knew how to give. Was she seeing a boy or girl? I didn't know. But of one thing I was certain, she was adrift in a moment unattached to any redeemable past or possible tomorrow. In the silence that followed, the ticking of her kitchen clock suddenly seemed unbearably loud.

Receive this: our hope, lost.

"Think it's in the gutter yet?" Wendy asked. It was now around seven and she had finished another bowl of soup and was standing at the window with her wine. The rain was still falling and the street in front of her house had started to flood. Through the darkness, her backyard garden had begun to look swampy and gross. If her grandma's hanky did end up being swept into the sewer system, she told me, it seemed appropriate, because that's where most miscarriages ended up anyway. She quietly chuckled. Why should she be different? "Yeah, why should you?" I almost shot back, but thought better of it. Instead, I joined her at the window.

Only a year earlier, I had watched the first pieces of my miscarrying body swirling down and away in the white porcelain toilet at work. I had held the tissue briefly in my hand when it first came out, uncertain what I was seeing, except that my body had made it but I couldn't keep it in me. My body wouldn't let me. If anyone cared to ask, I could give her a map of all the bathrooms at my school where, over the next three days, I had left similar pieces of myself: the women's room in the library and the one near my favorite lecture hall; there was also one in the administration building and one near our refectory. And when it wasn't tissue I left behind, it was blood, volumes of it. Rivers, it seemed, unstoppable rivers of red, death-carrying water, leaving a trail behind me. And I couldn't staunch its flow.

Now pieces of Wendy were probably following mine, only this time through streets, open and exposed, the safety of her grandmother's hanky an illusion. She turned and looked at me. "Looks like you need a blanket, too." She offered to get it and began to walk out of the room. "Seems like right now, it's the only thing holding me together."

How right she was. I had needed that blanket badly, something to hold me. In the ordinary course of my day, I have boundaries galore around me, some mental, some real. They are those rules or edges that let me know where I end and the world outside me begins. They are my borders, my skin, if you will. They hold me together. They also do many other things. They make me a safe teacher. They help me keep my work from completely invading my home. They let friends be friends, colleagues be colleagues, and my lover, a lover. And on a normal day, I enjoy the feel of these edges. They are, for the most part, comfortable. Like clothes, they adorn me in colors, textures, shapes, and tones that I desire. And I had particularly enjoyed imagining what my new set of mommy-to-be borders would look like: funky black Danskin maternity pants and a large, flowing, black silk top.

And then the blood had started flowing and I couldn't stop it. Nothing would keep it in or contain it, not my hands, not a sanitary pad or a tampon. Not my ardent will or my desired future. Not prayer nor a promise. Nothing.

Looking at that blood, in my underwear, running down my legs, gushing into toilet bowls, I felt as if the boundaries that contained me were, quite literally, coming undone. I couldn't hold inside me what needed to stay inside. I couldn't manage the edge between life and death. It was as if I was being strewn out into the world, unwilling, pieces of me everywhere. And with that unraveling came a profound sense of my own boundlessness: I wasn't just losing a pregnancy, I was losing myself.

To be selves, we need skin to contain us, clothes to warm us, and others who as others mark us as different and loved, the edges that hold us, that allow us to be something. Something.

"I found a great fleece one for you," I heard Wendy's voice coming from the hall.

It was then that I saw it: a small white thing floating through the garden, to the fence and then beyond.

Receive our body, ruptured; our blood, poured out.

By nine, we had finished two bottles of wine and Wendy was too drunk to walk straight, much less talk coherently. At least now she could properly blame herself. "I think it's time for you to get to bed, my dear." I had started taking our dishes to the sink.

"But I don't want to," she slurred.

"I'll help you."

"You can't. Don't you understand? You can't help me." Her flare for the dramatic was showing.

"I know. But I can at least get you up the stairs," I said with the slight edge of exasperation creeping into my voice. I hoped she would hear it.

"Watch me." With that, Wendy stood and swaggered towards the stairwell, and with stomping feet, heavy with determination and alcohol, she made her way up to the bedroom where she tumbled, fully dressed, onto the bed and curled up, fetal-like, again. There was no light on. Only the rain-blurred glimmer of an outside street lamp came through the window, casting shadows across the room's cluttered mess of clothes and books and tapers and teacups and vitamin bottles and herbs and blankets. The smell of incense was thick. Beside her bed, I could see where a recently burned candle had formed a puddle of red wax before finally going out. Had she spent the morning trying to find the right potion, the right essential oil, the right spell to stop it all? Wendy's sense of magic and wonder had always intrigued me, particularly when she had told me she was pregnant and the tarot cards had predicted it all.

Now as she lay drunk in the middle of her potion-filled chaos, that magic seemed like silly child's play. And her sense of wonder felt more pathetic than enchanting, more desperate than hopeful. But at least it was something, which is more than it felt like the church had given me.

Untangling the sheet covers piled at the foot of her bed, I tried to wrap her up warmly, like I was tucking in a child. But it was not one that was my own. Not the one I hadn't borne. Not the one whose future I had planned. Not the one whose nose I had already known. Not the one I would take to India and who would tend to my grave. Not the one I had bled out into the world, unable to protect. Not the one I couldn't save, the one I couldn't keep.

No, I was just tucking in a friend who held all of these same feelings now in her. My powerless, guilty Wendy; my friend unstuck in time, her body ruptured; my sister who in her dreams would probably search all night for those parts of herself surging towards the dark bowels of the city.

She reached out for my hand and pulled it tight into her. "Serene, I'm afraid to sleep. It's like I'm falling into death."

"But you're alive, Wendy."

Her fingers curled even more tightly around my fingers. "Could you do me one last favor? That oil on the dresser, the stuff in the small pink, glass bottle, could you put some on my forehead?"

I pulled my hand free and, in the darkness, I searched for the little bottle, finally finding it under a bra on her dresser top. It had spilled, soaking the soft white silk of her undergarment. My fingers rubbed across it. "This is all I could find." I came back to the bed and she turned her face up towards me. "On the forehead," she said, her eyes flat, her tongue thick.

"Wendy, this isn't going to give you a baby. You know that, don't you?" I probably shouldn't have said it, but I just didn't have the energy to begin a pointless fertility or pregnancy rite with her.

58

"You don't understand. I am not asking you to save a life. You're anointing the dead."

As my finger brushed her face, there, beneath me in the darkness of her room, I felt myself pulled into the horror of those words, that reality. Her body, my body, we were graves. No, we weren't the dying. We would live to see another day, for sure. But that day would be a haunted one for we also weren't simply in the world of the living, either. The site of the death we were grieving wasn't some car accident on the interstate or the cancer ward at the hospital. The space of this death wasn't a cross on a hillside where mothers wept at a distance. Nor was it some rock-hewn cave beyond the walls of Jerusalem. This death-site was inside us, deep in us. It was in a place even unknown to our own eyes, in a cavern from which we had believed a future would spring forth but from which only loss had issued. Not even death, for death supposes life and life was what we couldn't give. It was a tomb for the never-to-be: our bodies, ourselves.

Receive this: the grave that we are.

GIVING VOICE

Lift up your eyes round about and see;
they all gather, they come to you.
ISAIAH 49:18, RSV

It was around ten when I finally left Wendy's, the rain still pouring. I had done the dishes and put the soup away, rinsed out the wine bottles and thrown them in the recycling bin. Trying to restore order, I guess, but I think it was also my dread of going back to my own house where there was no child. A house where I was not the mother I had imagined I would be. A house that itself, at times, felt like a grave.

In the car, I stuck in a CD and decided to sit in Wendy's driveway for a time, just listening and waiting. After only a few lines of the singer's childlike plaintive voice, they came, the tears that had been there for a very long time. Curling around my steering wheel, I cried deep and hard about so many things.

Had I been able to be a minister to Wendy that day? Not in any conventional sense, I was certain. But then, how could I have been conventional when no convention existed to hold us? Throughout my time with her, I had kept running through the pages of Christian history and the rituals of the church in my mind, looking for something that might speak to us. Being a professor of theology and an ordained minister, I couldn't help it. It was my craft. And it was what Wendy had yearned for: a connection to old traditions like the Puritan piety of her grandmother or the Congregational steadiness of her mother, a connection she had sought in her candles and oils and old wives' tale wisdom. And just as that candle in her room seemed to have burned all the way down and then flickered out, so too my frantic search of Christianity seemed to have yielded nothing.

Oh, I knew lot of things I could have said, but didn't. I could have turned to Mary, the Mother of God herself, the truly annunciated one, the Blessed One. All day long, I had hoped she would visit us, either outside in the backyard or in Wendy's kitchen. I had awaited her inspiration. But each time she seemed to draw near, the particularity of my grief had pushed her back. Mary had a child and, yes, she had lost him. It seemed we should have been able to find solace in her on this score. But it didn't work. For thirty years, she watched him grow, saw him play, looked at his nose, ran her fingers through his hair. What a privilege, what blessings, when we had none. As far as I knew, she never lost agency, never came unhooked in time, and never bled her hope into a sewer. And her womb was never a grave.

And there were other theological things I could have said. I could have told her that tragedy and death were simply part of

God's fragile universe and we should bear up and accept our loss as just one more dimension of being human. But to say that would have seemed cold and uncaring, and as such, not true. Or, I could have promised her that this hoped-for child was waiting for her in heaven and that, one day, they would dwell together in God's presence. But if I had said this, I would have been lying. I simply didn't believe that all our miscarried hopes were wandering around in heaven waiting for mommy to show up.

I also could have said something about God not giving us anything we can't handle, invoking a controlling God who promises that everything will work for good, if we are just patient. But I didn't believe that God sent us suffering to test our faith or make us stronger. That wasn't the God of my faith.

But if these things weren't true, what was? Who was the God I believed in, the God I had hoped would touch us with grace, the God to whom I had spontaneously prayed in the backyard, the one who I hoped had heard all the mournful laments of these last tortured hours, the one I wanted so badly to hold me, here and now, in this cold, dark car?

I sat there and the tears kept coming as the singing continued. I reached up to wipe my nose and caught the scent of Wendy's anointing oil, still on my hands. How does one find hope when death is inside you, deep in your viscera, a part of your being, and yet you are not dead?

It was then that I saw it. Its truth was so expansive that it covered everything in my vision as it descended around me, taking the whole world into itself. A dark vision, it moved down towards the earth, pulling me with it. For centuries, the great theological minds of Christianity have struggled with a seemingly unanswerable question, an ancient quandary of faith. What happens in the Trinity when, on the cross, the Son of God dies? When he dies a complete death, not a partial one, not a fake one, but a full death as is the confession? All of him is gone, dead and buried.

What happens to that glorious communion of persons we call "God" when one of the three is lost to history? Do the other two cry for a while, get dressed up in black, and go to the funeral? Do they offer a toast to their lost friend, one struck down in the prime of his life by that awful killer "sin" or the devil? Or maybe they bide their time playing cards, knowing the resurrection is on its way? Do they grin secretly at each other, knowing it's all just a matter of time?

No, none of these happen.

We are told that the grief of this event is unlike any other known to us. Our ancient theologians tell us we can't extrapolate from our experience to it, for it is part of the divine mystery; it stretches beyond human imagination. Yet what is it we cannot imagine? The whole of Trinity, we are told, takes death into itself. Jesus doesn't die outside of God but in God, deep in the viscera of that holy tripartite union. Because the union is full, no part of God remains untouched by this death. It seeps into every corner of the whole body of persons. If this is true, then, yes, God becomes quite literally the site of dying. The Trinity is a grave, a dank tomb of death.[3]

In that cave where he is buried, that womb outside Jerusalem's walls, we find not only the body of Jesus, his flesh torn in tortured death, but also the tissue of a future that would never be. Buried with him is a dead hope. What dies is the hope carried by the disciples, the belief that the kingdom was coming, that the realm of justice was about to enter time, that a new age was dawning in which all our yearnings would be transformed into joy. On the cross, we encounter the death of an advent, an expectation.

So, too, in that dying, borders are unraveled, identities ripped open. Those lines that mark the edge distinguishing God from world, divine from human, immortal from enfleshed, they disintegrate before our eyes, not in the incarnation but in crucifixion. There, on the cross, the Trinity is ruptured, hemorrhaged, a blood-flow that will not stop. And in its wake, pieces of humanity's enfleshed hope lie scattered across space and time, sewer-bound, muddied.

The most haunting, troubled specter of all, however, is not just this bloodied dying but also the terrifying reality that the God who bears this death inside does not die, but lives to grieve another day. God is bereft of life and yet alive. This is the God who came to me in that dark descending vision, the God I supposedly could not fathom. There she was, in the garden, curled around Wendy, holding her. There she was.

The miscarrying woman, the mother whose child lies dead inside her, the sister betrayed by her own flesh as hope grows still in her womb, the friend who anoints her body for its journey to the grave, all these women, from ages past and on into our vast future, were with me in the car, and from the broken wisdom of their bodies and mine, I came to feel God anew, wrapped in her embrace.

And I heard her say, "I know, I know," as my tears continued.

Liturgies are strange things, particularly liturgies of mourning. Even stranger are the unrehearsed ones, those not-yet-born rituals that happen without planning or program, like the one that happened to Wendy and me that day. We certainly didn't plan it. I arrived with my ministerial hands empty and my panic full blown. Wendy met me with her cramping grief and her bloodied handkerchief. And then somehow, together, we stumbled into a ceremony strong enough to hold us.[4]

What we did that day, our litany, was not what we normally call a worship service or even more properly, a funeral. No, the sound and feel of it were far different from what we knew as regular Sunday morning church-time. Moreover, the meaning of our actions was elusive to us, at least in the moment. We did not think through what we did; no articulated theology guided us. It was more like we moved by instinct, as if creeping along a twisted path that our lifelong faith had carved out but then forgotten to explain; to follow, we had to stay close to the ground and slowly feel our way forward, our movements careful, primitive, and groping.

It began, I suppose, when she called and asked me to come and I showed up. That was our call to worship, our gathering of community: our invocation. And it ended when, late in the evening, I had helped Wendy into bed, full of wine and soup, wrapped in blankets, a towel between her legs, her head fragranced for death. Or perhaps it was ending here, in the car, my annunciation. And in between the beginning and the end, there was the backyard burial with its muddied clothes and fractured plea for help and our laments. In between were the hours-long kitchen conversation with its brothy food, dark red drink, and quietly shared agonies: rituals that ebbed and flowed with the shifting rhythms of our awful wrestling. A wrestling with bodies that had betrayed us, a life that had been denied us, and a God we were not certain knew how to speak to us. A wrestling we undertook together; a wrestling shaped, at its core, by a litany older than our invocation and benediction; a litany of testifying and witnessing. What did it sound like? It sounded like the Trinity.

Their voices are guttural; their body motions, slumped and heavy; their patterned tones, disjointed, a groan, a sway, the unconscious but methodical building of the softly pounding rhythm of a rage-yet-seen, a tapping foot on a kitchen floor, growing louder, pounding, and then a dying beat, a collective sigh. And once again, long silence, long, thick silence, broken perhaps by the rustle of a blanket pulled more tightly around cold shoulders. Sometimes by a barely audible melody slipping out unawares when the mind stumbles upon a remembered childhood song of comfort or a hymn first heard at an uncle's graveside. Several lines drift out and then slip away again into a silence now laden with memories too delicate for speech.

And then speech comes, but not in sermonic form. It's there in the longed-for sound of that half-spoken, half-whispered chant of "I know. I know. It's okay." Words whose meaning rests not in the trivial sense of an already-known knowledge or the promise that all is well or soon will be, but rather in their power to affirm presence and hold sadness.

If sacred actions yearn for particular kinds of spaces, then mourning begs not for sky nor water nor ornate temples nor lean granite pillars but for earth: simple, deep, and dark brown, saturated with age, dank and full of mystery. Grief seeks earth.

Looking back on that ceremony now, six years later, I realize I wasn't as alone as I felt that day. I had a church that had taught me to grieve with God, and a community of lovers who had taught me how to say "I know," and a heart softened by grace that was supple enough to take the weight of her body as it leaned into me. And most of all I had Wendy, a sister who would go with me to the grave. Two women. A tomb. And there with us, the most blessed gift of all, the dark, miscarrying, aching Trinity that held us.

COMFORT FOR WOMEN WHO HAVE HAD A MISCARRIAGE
Martin Luther, 1542

*A final word—it often happens that devout parents, particularly the wives,
have sought consolation from us because they have suffered such agony and
heartbreak in child-bearing when, despite their best intentions and against
their will, there was a premature birth or miscarriage and their child died at
birth or was born dead.*

*One ought not to frighten or sadden such mothers by harsh words
because it was not due to their carelessness or neglect that the birth of the
child went off badly. One must make a distinction between them and those
females who resent being pregnant, deliberately neglect their child, or go so
far as to strangle or destroy it. This is how one ought to comfort them.*

*First, inasmuch as one cannot and ought not know the hidden judg-
ment of God in such a case—why, after every possible care had been taken,
God did not allow the child to be born alive and be baptized—these mothers
should calm themselves and have faith that God's will is always better than
ours, though it may seem otherwise to us from our human point of view.
They should be confident that God is not angry with them or with others
who are involved. Rather is this a test to develop patience. We well know that
these cases have never been rare since the beginning and that Scripture also
cites them as examples, as in Psalm 58[:8], and St. Paul calls himself an*
abortivum, *a misbirth or one untimely born [1 Cor. 15:8].*

*Second, because the mother is a believing Christian it is to be hoped
that her heartfelt cry and deep longing to bring her child to be baptized will
be accepted by God as an effective prayer. It is true that a Christian in deepest despair does not dare to name, wish, or hope for the help (as it seems to
him) which he would wholeheartedly and gladly purchase with his own life
were that possible, and in doing so thus find comfort. However, the words*

of Paul, Romans 8[:26–27], properly apply here: "Likewise the Spirit helps us in our weakness; for we do not know how to pray as we ought (that is, as was said above, we dare not express our wishes), rather the Spirit himself intercedes for us mightily with sighs too deep for words. And he who searches the heart knows what is the mind of the Spirit," etc. Also Ephesians 3[:20], "Now to him who by the power at work within us is able to do far more abundantly than all that we ask or think."

One should not despise a Christian person as if he were a Turk, a pagan, or a godless person. He is precious in God's sight and his prayer is powerful and great, for he has been sanctified by Christ's blood and anointed with the Spirit of God. Whatever he sincerely prays for, especially in the unexpressed yearning of his heart, becomes a great, unbearable cry in God's ears. God must listen, as he did to Moses, Exodus 14[:15], "Why do you cry to me?" even though Moses couldn't whisper, so great was his anxiety and trembling in the terrible troubles that beset him. His sighs and the deep cry of his heart divided the Red Sea and dried it up, led the children of Israel across, and drowned Pharaoh with all his army [Exod. 14:26–28], etc. This and even more can be accomplished by a true, spiritual longing. Even Moses did not know how or for what he should pray—not knowing how the deliverance would be accomplished—but his cry came from his heart.

Isaiah did the same against King Sennacherib [Isa. 37:4] and so did many other kings and prophets who accomplished inconceivable and impossible things by prayer, to their astonishment afterward. But before that they would not have dared to expect or wish so much of God. This means to receive things far higher and greater than we can understand or pray for, as St. Paul says, Ephesians 3[:20], etc. Again, St. Augustine declared that his mother was praying, sighing, and weeping for him, but did not desire anything more than that he might be converted from the errors of the Manicheans and become a Christian [Confessions, 5.8]. Thereupon

God gave her not only what she desired but, as St. Augustine puts it, her "chiefest desire" (cardinem desideriieius), that is, what she longed for with unutterable sighs—that Augustine become not only a Christian but also a teacher above all others in Christendom. Next to the apostles Christendom has none that is his equal.

Who can doubt that those Israelite children who died before they could be circumcised on the eighth day were yet saved by the prayers of their parents in view of the promise that God willed to be their God. God (they say) has not limited his power to the sacraments, but has made a covenant with us through his word. Therefore we ought to speak differently and in a more consoling way with Christians than with pagans or wicked people (the two are the same), even in such cases where we do not know God's hidden judgment. For he says and is not lying, "All things are possible to him who believes" [Mark 9:23], even though they have not prayed, or expected, or hoped for what they would have wanted to see happen. Enough has been said about this. Therefore one must leave such situations to God and take comfort in the thought that he surely has heard our unspoken yearning and done all things better than we could have asked.

In summary, see to it that above all else you are a true Christian and that you teach a heartfelt yearning and praying to God in true faith, be it in this or any other trouble. Then do not be dismayed or grieved about your child or yourself, and know that your prayer is pleasing to God and that God will do everything much better than you can comprehend or desire. "Call upon me," he says in Psalm 50[:15], "in the day of trouble; I will deliver you, and you shall glorify me." For this reason one ought not straightway condemn such infants for whom and concerning whom believers and Christians have devoted their longing and yearning and praying. Nor ought one to consider them the same as others for whom no faith, prayer, or yearning are expressed on the part of Christians and believers. God intends that his promise *and our prayer or yearning which is grounded in that promise should not be disdained or rejected, but be highly valued and esteemed. I have said it before and preached it often enough: God accomplishes much through the faith and longing of another, even a stranger, even though there is still no personal faith. But this is given through the channel of another's intercession, as in the gospel Christ raised the widow's son at Nain because of the prayers of his mother apart from the faith of the son [Luke 7:11–17]. And he freed the little daughter of the Canaanite woman from the demon through the faith of the mother apart from the daughter's faith [Matt. 15:22–28]. The same was true of the king's son, John 4[:46-53], and of the paralytic and many others of whom we need not say anything here.*

—Translated from German by James Raun

FOUR *comfort*

K R I S T E N   E.   K V A M

In July of 1994, my husband and I were thrilled to learn that I
was pregnant with our second child. It seemed such a wonderful time to be expecting another family member. Our daughter
had just celebrated her fourth birthday and she was anticipating life
as a big sister with great joy. I was in my third year of teaching;
course schedules for the spring semester had been juggled so that I
could have a maternity leave after the baby would be born in
March. My husband was pastoring a small congregation and his
Calvinist sensibilities shone through in his sense that my pregnancy
at this time in our lives was truly a gift from God. Our confidence
and our hope grew with every passing week. We had no reasons for

anxiety beyond the normal apprehensions because the pregnancy with our daughter had been so smooth. My body was strong, and I had learned to listen to it and appreciate its strength in new ways.

In late November, when I was just days away from finishing the twenty-fourth week, a cessation of fetal movement alerted us that something was not right. We tried suppressing our fears, but the skills of the medical community confirmed them: our awaited baby, Amanda Lois, was not coming.

I am not certain when I remembered Martin Luther's (1483–1546) text entitled "Comfort for Women Who Have Had a Miscarriage" (hereafter referred to as Letter of Comfort). I do know that even after I recalled this short treatise, it was months before I was able to look at it. Reading about grief and loss, about miscarriage and stillbirth, was beyond my capacities for many months. Now, years later, having studied this sixteenth-century text, I have come to believe that through it, Luther offers a significant legacy to contemporary Christians as we consider our responses to reproductive loss. Luther's Letter of Comfort continues to offer solace to those of us who suffer agony and heartbreak in childbearing. It also provides important resources for contemporary Christians when we consider ways our faith community could respond to those who grieve the miscarriage, stillbirth, and infant death of awaited children.

MISCARRIAGE

That Luther penned this short text was merely by chance. In 1541, pastor John Bugenhagen (1484–1558) wrote an interpretation of Psalm 29 and showed this text to his close friend and colleague Martin Luther. He may have wanted Luther simply to read his treatise; Luther instead responded by suggesting how Bugenhagen could improve the text. Bugenhagen's use of the phrase "little children" had prompted Luther to recommend the addition of a discussion directed to parents who knew the agonies of encountering death in childbearing. Although Bugenhagen chose not to follow his good friend's instruction—perhaps he did not see himself as equipped for drafting such a discussion—he was willing to add an appendix to his text if Luther would write it. Luther thought the project so important that he accepted and wrote an eight-paragraph appendix. In an ironic turn of events, Luther's Letter of Comfort has outlived the book to which it originally had been attached.

Although I live four centuries after the women to whom Luther addressed his letter, I am not so distant from his original audience. Luther describes them in his opening: "A final word—it often happens that devout parents, particularly the wives, have sought consolation from us because they have suffered such agony and heartbreak in child-bearing when, despite their best intentions and against their will, there was a premature birth or miscarriage and their child died at birth or was born dead." Clearly, Luther had in mind expectant parents whose pregnancies had been desired and wanted. Their child's death occurred, as he said, "despite their best intentions and against their will." His description reminded me of all I had done to ensure the well-being of Amanda Lois. I had taken all the known precautions: established a relationship with an obstetrician, swallowed prenatal vitamins, and avoided alcohol. I thought of other women who, fearful of an impending miscarriage, willingly took to their beds for days, weeks, and even months in hopes of preventing pregnancy loss. Yet despite our efforts, death came.

Luther goes on to distinguish the women he is addressing from those "females who resent being pregnant, deliberately neglect their child, or go so far as to strangle or destroy it." What I appreciate in his distinction is the way that it directs our thinking to once-expectant parents who grieve the end of pregnancies they had desired. Contemporary Christian communities have spent considerable energy thinking about how they should respond to unwanted pregnancies. Luther directs our attention to a group that often escapes our theological attention: those who mourn the loss of hoped-for children.

We should not assume, however, that the use of "miscarriage" in the title of Luther's text is the same as our current usage. We commonly use the word "miscarriage" to indicate spontaneous pregnancy losses that occur from the time of conception to soon after the twentieth week. Historical studies help us see how unlikely it is that Luther was thinking about losses that occurred so early. For one thing, determinations of when a woman was considered pregnant were very different in Luther's time. In the sixteenth century, the onset of pregnancy was determined by the expectant mother herself on the basis of her experience of her body. "Quickening" (the experience of fetal movement) was understood to be the decisive factor in knowing that she was pregnant. For a first-time mother, this experience might not occur with any clarity until the fourth or fifth month after conception. This sense of pregnancy's onset differs sharply from our practices of over-the-counter pregnancy tests and their early evaluations.

Historians also help us understand that "quickening" was perceived to have much greater significance than the experience we commonly describe as the baby moving or "kicking." For premodern persons, these stirrings were understood as the beginnings of distinctively human life, as the time when God gave the baby a soul. Quickening literally was a sign of "en-soulment." People during the sixteenth century understood that life forms have bodies and even spirits; they spoke of plants having "vegetative" spirits. Having a soul, in their view, was the hallmark of the human person and only human beings were understood to have souls. Moreover, en-soulment was understood to occur within the womb as part of the process of the development of human life. God gives each of us a soul, an *anima*, as part of our "animation," our quickening in the wombs of our mothers.[1]

Therefore the use of the term "miscarriage" in the title of Luther's text more closely corresponds to our use of the term "stillbirth." Although there is no absolute or rigid line dividing these two forms of pregnancy loss, we tend to think of miscarriage as happening earlier in a pregnancy than premodern persons and we think of stillbirth as the cessation of fetal development after the fourth month. Luther would have been writing his Letter of Comfort to women whose pregnancy losses had occurred at least four or five months after conception or, as he wrote, when "there was a premature birth or miscarriage and their child died at birth or was born dead."

This variance in sensibility does not prohibit the Letter from offering solace to persons whose experience of loss has occurred earlier than Luther would have envisioned. His attention was directed to those who, in his words, have sought consolation "because they have suffered such agony and heartbreak in childbearing." Detailing whether this agony is because the expectant parents had lived in anticipation of a child for seven months, seven weeks, or seven days seems to be a misplaced concern for calculation amid a heartfelt, and even heartsick, desire for consolation.

Luther is quick to offer such consolation. Already in the second paragraph of his letter he writes: "One ought not to frighten or sadden such mothers by harsh words because it was not due to their carelessness or neglect that the birth of the child went off badly." This admonition serves as a negative criterion and all means of solace should be measured according to this standard. If what we say or do frightens or saddens the once-expectant parents, these means are not effective agents of consolation. Our words and our actions are to be measured by their effects rather than our intentions. If they do not console the grief-stricken, they are not words of comfort, no matter our motivation.

Luther's admonition stands against currents in his own cultural context. He lived in an age that had expansive notions of women's influence on their pregnancies. For example, it was commonly believed that if a pregnant woman saw blood, she would bear a redheaded child, or if she had an encounter with a grave-yard, her baby would be injured.

We may smile at these premodern ideas, yet an exaggerated estimate of women's responsibility for the outcome of their preg-nancies persists in our own day. Contemporary women who grieve a miscarriage or stillbirth often are quick to assume re-sponsibility for the loss by saying: "I shouldn't have drunk that cup of coffee; I shouldn't have lifted that chair; I shouldn't have run to catch the bus; I shouldn't have flown on that airplane." Medical personnel scoff at such litanies. But once-expectant women, desperate for a reason for their loss, will often cast about for causes, even at the expense of their own peace of mind. Sadly, given our culture's perception of the individual's control over their fates, other voices may join in: "Why did you have that glass of wine? Why did you keep attending your exercise class? Why didn't you keep that doctor's appointment?" Luther's injunction that "it was not due to their carelessness or neglect" stands strong against the impulse of grieving parents and tactless neighbors to create blame where none is deserved. For Luther, we are not the ultimate arbiters of our fates, and we ought not compound the sorrow and fears of grieving women by holding them culpable for pregnancy loss.

After his admonition, Luther focuses his attention on specific instructions for how to offer comfort. Here, he organizes his re-marks to make two points: his first point concerns the relation-ship between God and the grieving mother; his second concerns the mother's desire for a relationship between God and the child she was expecting. If length of discussion indicates interest, Luther's major preoccupation was with the second point. Yet his first point deserves our attention because it still carries weight: "First, inasmuch as one cannot and ought not know the hidden judgment of God in such a case—why, after every possible care had been taken, God did not allow the child to be born alive and be baptized—these mothers should calm themselves and have faith that God's will is always better than ours, though it may seem otherwise to us from our human point of view. They should be confident that God is not angry with them or with others who are involved. Rather is this a test to develop patience."

In this paragraph Luther sets the relationship between the grieving mother and God as the central focus of attention. While understanding and describing this particular relationship provides his focus, the advice he gives is applicable to all who would encounter this mother or speak about her. The key to this discussion is Luther's emphasis that bereaved mothers should, as he states, "calm themselves and have faith that God's will is always better than ours." The rest of the paragraph demonstrates what Luther means by having faith in God's will.

Recognizing that grieving parents will seek to find meaning in their pregnancy loss, Luther warns against some ways of proceeding in the quest for meaning. Most notably, he cautions against explaining miscarriage and stillbirth by God's anger, saying: "They should be confident that God is not angry with them or with others who are involved." A friend of mine who facilitates discussions on infertility and spirituality reports that the number one concern of the assembled individuals is "maybe God is punishing me, maybe God is angry with me." Some have even heard family and friends suggest that infertility is God's way of telling them that they shouldn't be parents.

Luther goes on to caution against devising any explanations at all when he stresses the "hidden judgment of God," saying "one cannot and ought not know the hidden judgment of God in such a case." In this statement I hear an important watchword against well-intended but hurtful comments such as "there must have been something wrong with your baby." After Amanda Lois died, I heard this from many well-meaning people. No doubt they were trying to console me with the possibility that we, and Amanda

Lois, were being spared a harder future; but in the face of our loss these words rang hollow and even cavalier. Luther's agnosticism concerning God's decision making encourages us to hesitate to offer explanations for what needs to remain incomprehensible. One cannot and ought not know the hidden judgment of God.

Luther, however, falters in following his own advice, and this is a matter of consternation for me. Instead of adhering to his initial comments that God's judgment "cannot and ought not" be known in relation to miscarriage, Luther verges on a rationale for the inexplicable when he describes the pregnancy loss as "a test to develop patience." He does not say that persons might *use* their experience as a way to develop patience. Instead he says that it *is* such a test. This conveys the impression that he has discerned God's judgment and knows that God wills that this once-expectant mother and father need to become more patient. I find this move theologically unfortunate. Luther is on sounder ground when he refrains from speculating about divine reasons for human tragedies. His opening statement at the beginning of this paragraph bears repeating: "one cannot and ought not know the hidden judgment of God in such a case."

BAPTISM

The power of Luther's thinking comes to the fore when he responds to a major source of anguish for Christian parents of a miscarried or stillborn child, and that is baptism. Students and friends of mine who are pastors and hospital chaplains often provide pastoral care to couples who have lost an awaited child through miscarriage or stillbirth.[2] When circumstances have made baptism impossible, they know this will cause agony for many parents to whom they minister. Some once-expectant parents will be anxious about the fate of their expected child. Others may not worry about their hoped-for child's future, yet will find themselves casting about for a ritual to mark the momentous event that has occurred. They want a ritual for the awaited child's sake as well as for their own, something that acknowledges the expected child and that acknowledges their grief. They long for a way to symbolize the life and the loss.

Anxiety about the eternal fate of a miscarried or stillborn child was more intense in Luther's day than our own and Luther himself had a strong sense of how crucial baptism was to a person's well-being. A passage in his 1529 Large Catechism displays his estimation of baptism's significance: "No greater jewel, therefore, can adorn our body and soul than baptism, for through it we become completely holy and blessed, which no other kind of life and no work on earth can acquire."[3] With such ultimate importance placed on baptism, parents would have reason to ask what the otherworldly fate would be of quickened babies who died before or shortly after they were born and what the eternal destiny of these babies would be.

In the letter's fourth paragraph, Luther turns to such concerns, and this complex of issues occupies him for the rest of the Letter. Early in the church's life, baptism was performed only at Easter. But both the frequency and the timing of baptism underwent considerable change during the medieval era. By the fourteenth century the common practice was to baptize infants soon after they were born. By then, the dominant theology of original sin, with its consequent prediction of hellfire for all who were unbaptized, required the sacrament to follow quickly after a child was born, often within a few days of birth. In fact, in stark contrast to our preference for the immediate family's involvement in their baby's baptism, mothers usually were not present when their children were baptized. Mothers would have been confined to the childbed until they had participated in a postnatal rite of purification and reintegration called "churching." Usually it was the midwife who would carry the newborn to the church to be baptized.[4]

Prior to Luther, the medieval church offered comfort to expectant parents suffering the anguish of miscarriage, stillbirth, and infant death through its teaching known as *limbus infantum* or *limbus puerorum* ("children's limbo"), which provided a significant way to assure those who were grieving prenatal loss that the child did not suffer the torments of hell. Just as we use the word "limbo" to speak of being between two options, *limbus infantum* was portrayed as an intermediate state. Scholastic teaching presented it as a place between the beautiful and eternal joy of heaven and the unspeakable and eternal suffering of hell. Souls who died before baptism were incapable of entering heaven because they had not been cleansed of their participation in original sin. Yet newborns and the unborn had not participated in actual sin so they need not suffer the pangs of hell. In fact, most teachings stressed that these children would not suffer at all. They would spend eternal life in complete natural happiness; their deprivation was that they would not know the supernatural happiness of heaven.

It is striking that Luther never mentions the *limbus infantum* in his Letter of Comfort. Certainly his focus on baptism and the mother's desire for a relationship between God and the expected child would have been an apt time for him to discuss this teaching, and we know from his other writings, some from this same year, that Luther was sharply critical of this theory of limbo. He scorned it as "nothing but dreams and human inventions." So why be silent about this in his Letter? It would have been an opportune time to speak out and encourage persons to conform their imaginations and thought with biblical teaching and evangelical doctrine!

As I've pondered this absence, I have come to conclude that Luther's silence offers its own distinctive witness. It seems clear that Luther would know that teachings about a children's limbo would have been an important source of consolation for many grieving parents. His decision not to criticize this doctrine in the Letter of Comfort means that he did not feel compelled to critique it at every occasion and not mentioning it would allow this measure of comfort to remain a possibility for the grief stricken who were so inclined. Perhaps he thought that another time would be better to educate them away from this questionable teaching. For whatever reason, his willingness to leave some things unsaid is a useful reminder to us today. Sometimes the church stands better with those who grieve by being silent.

Luther offers an important alternative to limbo as a significant way to console bereft parents. Intriguingly, he states: "because the mother is a believing Christian it is to be hoped that her heartfelt cry and deep longing to bring her child to be baptized will be accepted by God as an effective prayer." What does Luther mean by this?

I was taught that according to Luther, baptism is necessary for salvation. Perhaps I learned this in that laboratory of Lutheran doctrine: confirmation class. But it isn't only children confirmed at Zion Lutheran Church in Litchfield, Minnesota, who think that Luther held to this view. The entry on "Infant Salvation" in a standard reference volume, the *New Schaff-Herzog Encyclopedia of Religious Knowledge,* demonstrates that attributing the necessity of baptism to Luther is more widespread than the congregation where I was raised. This entry describes Huldrych Zwingli (1484–1531) as "the first to enter the lists against the theory of the necessity of baptism to infant salvation." It then states: "Luther, on the other hand, taught the necessity of baptism to salvation, and this doctrine is part of the Lutheran Creed, involving baptismal regeneration."[5]

The Letter of Comfort, however, undercuts the certainty of this estimation. In it, Luther appeals to the example of Israelite children who died before they were circumcised on the eighth day. He asks, "Who can doubt that those Israelite children . . . were . . . saved by the prayers of their parents in view of the promise that God willed to be their God." He concludes: "God (they say) has not limited his power to the sacraments, but has made a covenant with us through his word." This example and this statement illustrate Luther's profound understanding of the bounty and freedom of God's grace.

How powerful Luther's discussion must have been to those who grieved that their awaited children had died before they had been baptized! It assures them, and us, that God's saving love, though ordinarily given through the sacraments, can reach us beyond the bounds of the sacraments.

PRAYER

Tucked within Luther's discussion of baptism and the Israelite children, I find another avenue of comfort for those grieving reproductive loss. He characterizes the once-expectant mother's "heartfelt cry and deep longing" as "an effective prayer." For those of us who have found infertility, miscarriage, and stillbirth devastating to our prayer life, this is good news indeed. Many women speak of being unable to pray during their starkest days and nights of struggling with reproduction. Others lament their confusion over what is acceptable to pray for in this time. When facing stillbirth and miscarriage, is it appropriate to pray for the soul of the awaited baby? When facing infertility, is it all right to pray for a baby or even to pray for a healthy baby?

Luther moves from reference to the mother's "heartfelt cry and deep longing" into a powerful discussion of the nature and effects of prayer. He continues: "It is true that a Christian in deepest despair does not dare to name, wish, or hope for the help . . . which he would wholeheartedly and gladly purchase with his own life were that possible, and in doing so thus find comfort." Luther realized that grief often takes away an ability to pray. Sometimes we think that this inability is caused by a sense of betrayal for what has happened and our anger that God did not stop it. But a different obstacle appears to have been in Luther's mind. His text emphasizes what we might call "a loss of language." Consider again his description: "A Christian in deepest despair does not dare to name, wish, or hope" for the help that would offer comfort. A few sentences later Luther wrote of "the unexpressed yearning" of a person's heart and how it becomes, in his words, "a great, unbearable cry in God's ears."

Persons who have experienced reproductive loss know a profound kind of bewilderment. They have not only lost a longed for child, they have lost the ability to articulate their life and to imagine their hopes. Infertility, miscarriage, and stillbirth can catapult us to the edge of language, and leave us bereft of words. Texts in the area of reproductive loss signal this fracturing with such titles as *When Birth Means Death, Silence in the Nursery, Counting to Zero, Ended Beginnings,* and *When Hello Means Goodbye.*

How do you pray when you have no language? My experience of loss brought new insights into what it means to be part of a community in prayer. Being prayed for can mean that prayer is being offered in your stead, precisely because you are unable to pray. "Being lifted up" by the community in prayer can mean that you are not only named in a petition but also that the community is praying on your behalf when you cannot "name, wish, or hope" for what would bring you comfort. I see this understanding of prayer at work in a letter Luther wrote about his daughter Magdalena's death. In this letter Luther told his friend about the sorrow he and his wife, Katie, had experienced. He then asked the friend to "give thanks to God in our stead." This request urges friends and family, church members and Christian communities to stand in the place of the bereft and pray on their behalf, knowing that the grieving themselves may not have words for forming their own prayers.[6]

The crucial point in the Letter of Comfort, however, is not that grief often takes away our ability to pray; it is rather that God hears and responds to desires we cannot articulate. Luther lifts up the example of Moses to encourage Christians to recognize how God hears and responds to our unspoken prayers. Luther's description is lengthy but deserves a careful reading: "God must listen, as he did to Moses, [in] Exodus 14[:15], 'Why do you cry to me?' even though Moses couldn't whisper, so great was his anxiety and trembling in the terrible troubles that beset him. His sighs and the deep cry of his heart divided the Red Sea and dried it up, led the children of Israel across, and drowned Pharaoh with all his army. . . . Even Moses did not know how or for what he should pray—not knowing how the deliverance would be accomplished—but his cry came from his heart."

It is moving to hear how Luther portrays Moses as dividing the Red Sea by "his sighs and the deep cry of his heart." Luther continues his stress on the efficacy of unspoken desire in the next paragraph, as he highlights how the lives of figures like the biblical prophet Isaiah and Monica, the mother of Augustine of Hippo (354–430), testify to the ways that unimagined accomplishments arise out of "unutterable sighs."

Luther's Letter of Comfort encourages contemporary Christians to be attentive to persons who have suffered "agony and heartbreak in child-bearing" and to offer theological reflection as a vital form of comfort. In these eight paragraphs, Luther provides an important way to proceed. On the one hand, his letter encourages us to recognize and acknowledge the agony of the loss. But, on the other hand, it urges us to do so with a kind of imaginative reticence. His suggestions are significant for shaping contemporary practices and attitudes, especially because of our discomfort with grief and our sense of privacy concerning pregnancy loss. Following Luther's lead, heartfelt yearnings for which we have neither words nor concepts rightfully remain inarticulate and unexpressed. We need not over-conceptualize our responses to loss. As Luther said, "Even Moses did not know how or for what he should pray."

The point remains, for Luther and for us: God's grace alone offers comfort. And it is a grace that will work effects beyond the hopes we can imagine. Whatever grief besets us, we should take it to God in prayer. We can offer to God the fears and worries that plague our hearts, even the ones for which we have no words. According to Brother Martin's letter, even when we are inarticulate, God, in God's bounteous and free mercy, hears and responds to our deepest needs.

LAMENT PSALM FORTY-SEVEN

Ann Weems, 1995

I stand at your empty table,

O Holy One,

and ask to be fed.

But there is no bread,

no wine,

no priest.

Is there no one to

minister

to me?

Is there no place

at the table

for

damaged hearts

and

scarred souls?

Do you not invite

everyone who believes?

I believe.

O God,

I believe.

In spite of an empty table,

I believe.

In spite of those who laugh

at me as I wait

for you,

I believe.

In spite of evidence

to the contrary

that they scream

in my face,

I will stand at your empty table,

and wait

until you come,

your arms full of bread,

the wine splashing

as you walk.

Come, O Holy One,

and feed me.

FIVE *faith*

LINDA A. MERCADANTE

As a little girl, I loved playing with my dolls, but I didn't think much about having real children. I expected to have them, as did every other girl I knew, but I was more concerned with who I was than whom I would produce. I was the child of a Catholic-Jewish marriage who was not given a clear religious identity, and my life quest has been to unite faith and family. Infertility became the catalyst that made me redefine that quest entirely.

My Catholic father was an Italian immigrant, my Jewish mother the child of Austrian and Russian immigrants. They married during World War II over much familial opposition. Perhaps because of this, my parents did not practice their individual faiths and I was not told much of my religious background. But, growing up, I wanted God in my life and I wanted answers to the big questions I found I could not ask at home. This drive was so strong that in middle childhood I decided to become Catholic. Although I was surprised at the trouble this caused my parents, it did feel satisfying to have a faith identity.

Most of the time I had to go to church by myself, and I soon realized this situation was rather unusual. It became hard to see other children going to Mass with their parents, while I walked there, worshiped, and came home alone. It was not just implicitly, but also explicitly that I got the message that faith and family should be united. Sermons often focused on the importance of the family, and the motto "The family that prays together, stays together" seemed to be everywhere in mid-twentieth century America. While I knew it was futile to hope I would ever sit with my parents in church, someday I expected to have my own family and we would worship and celebrate together.

KINSHIP

But while the church at that time focused much attention on the nuclear family, it also communicated a wider vision. Nascent within the biblical texts, liturgy, and homilies, I heard a promise about adoption into God's family. I learned that people of faith have a transcendent connection beyond blood ties. I heard a strong message that we are to welcome outsiders and strangers and that they are included in God's graceful plan.

According to the *Baltimore Catechism,* we were meant to be a faith family: "Neighbor . . . means every human being, no matter where he lives or what his color, learning, manners, etc., for every human being in the world is a child of God and has been redeemed by Our Lord. Therefore every child of God is my neighbor, and even more—he is my brother; for God is his father and mine also, and if he is good enough for God to love, he should be good enough for me."[1]

At Mass, portions of the scriptures were always read. From them I learned that all of us were equal, "no longer strangers and sojourners, but . . . fellow citizens with the saints and members of the household of God" (Eph. 2:19 RSV). The stories I heard about Jesus showed he did not privilege biological family, but those who believed in him. For instance, when Jesus' family came for him, he said, "Who are my mother and my brothers? . . . Whoever does the will of God is my brother and sister and mother" (Mk. 3:33, 35). There was even a justification for someone like me, who felt guilty about causing disruption in the family. Although I loved my parents, it was some comfort to hear Jesus say that the one "whoever loves father or mother more than me is not worthy of me" (Matt. 10:37).

Over time, it dawned on me that family with God wasn't about blood ties but about love bonds; no one was born into this family, all were adopted. It wasn't that something was wrong with the biological family, but that God had an even deeper type of connection in mind for us. I was attracted to this vision without fully understanding it. Yet claiming a faith tradition did not automatically create a faith family for me. Aside from the occasional word from an usher, the nuns' teaching during my two years of catechism class, and the anonymous advice of the priest in the confessional, I had no significant contact with church members. The pledge of inclusion was not being fulfilled. Yet where else was I to go? This seemed to be the only place that promised community, purpose, and a higher vision of connection than was possible through biological ties.

During my young adult years I became a part of a Protestant Christian community in Europe that reawakened and refocused my spiritual and family needs. Here I met Christians who honored my dual background. I began to read the Bible for myself, starting in the Old Testament and working my way forward. After a month of reading and questioning, I had a profound conversion experience. I realized that Jesus not only was and remained a Jew, but did not repudiate his background. Instead, he came to fulfill it. Jews and Christians were meant to be one family of God, not two separated peoples. For the first time, I felt like a whole person.

I appreciated the Protestant emphasis on "the priesthood of believers" and its teachings that we needed no mediator to God, could read scripture for ourselves and trust the inspiration of the Holy Spirit. While I was among this community, the family of faith seemed a reality. While these people saw the nuclear family as important, they insisted it was only a building block for the larger family of God. Outsiders, singles, older people were all respected and integrally included. It was accepted that God gifted people in different ways, but that all were necessary to the body of Christ. For the first time, I felt a full member of the church regardless of my family status.

It also became clear that the biological family was not an end in itself. Instead, it was a base of service to a larger good and to a common goal that ultimately transcended biological kinship. Nor was the church an end in itself. Instead, it was a means of God's grace and a place of healing and growth. By focusing on faith ties, love, and long-term commitment, we were moving towards the vision of God's new creation. In this community I glimpsed a vision of how a group of disparate people could become family to each other. The bonds we were forging were meant to last into eternity.

Not everything was perfect, however. In spite of their intentions, these Christians often elevated the actual nuclear family to undue proportions. Likewise, their insistence on male leadership clashed with the freedom I saw promised by the gospel. When scripture said we were new creations in Christ, I saw no gender ranking. When Galatians 3:28 (RSV) said, "There is neither Jew nor Greek, there is neither slave nor free, there is neither male nor female; for you are all one in Christ Jesus. And if you are Christ's, then you are Abraham's offspring, heirs according to promise," I saw the old dividing walls torn down.

But these Christians insisted God only offered two choices for a woman. She could marry and assume a domestic ministry under the authority of her husband, or she could remain single and choose a more outward, freer service, but still under male authority in the church. I didn't know enough theology to argue with them successfully, yet I was feeling a call from God that transcended these limits. This frustration motivated me to study the Bible for myself with all the academic tools I could manage to acquire.

Inspired and challenged, I returned to the United States, changed my career path, and enrolled in graduate school. I pursued each question, and learned more about church history, exegesis, Greek and Hebrew, and especially theology. I discovered a love of theology, a call to ordination, and a vocation for seminary teaching. I married someone who seemed to have the same religious commitment. It felt wonderful to have a partner in the faith and I felt complete as the church and fellow students became family for us. Soon the desire for a child began to grow. It seemed a natural outpouring of the love we shared. It was not essential to our happiness but it promised to augment it.

Our desire was somewhat analogous to God's creative act. From my theological study, I realized that God did not need to create; the divine integrity and fulfillment of the triune God was inherently complete. But divine love simply overflows. It is the nature of love that it wants to be shared. Creation, and thus reproduction, was a way to share and spread the divine love. From my study, I learned that while the inner-trinitarian relationships already modeled perfect integrity and fulfillment, we as humans are only "en route." We are being remade in God's image through Christ. In the meantime, we could experience a foretaste of this communion in the church. Our family could be a link in the larger family of God.

How ironic, then, given this expanded vision that we should find out we were infertile. The desire that faith brought to fruition, biology could not fulfill. It was a terrible blow to realize that we would not sit in church with the offspring of our love. I would not give birth to the child who naturally included the Jewish and Christian sides I had struggled so hard to integrate. My husband would not fit in with his six Catholic sisters and their large broods. We would not produce the child that the jeweler who crafted our wedding rings had predicted would be so beautiful. After much time, testing, and money; many tears and procedures; by our early thirties we came to terms with the fact that we were not going to have biological children.

ADOPTION

But we still wanted a family. Counseling and the meetings of a support group for couples with infertility problems helped us accept our situation and move to other alternatives. Several of my cousins had adopted children and were very happy. We applied and were accepted by an adoption agency, but five more years passed while we were on the waiting list. The entire process, from first diagnosis of infertility to holding the lovely five-week-old we named David, had taken nearly ten years. Bringing David home was as happy an event as any birth could have been, and maybe more.

This long process made a deep impression on me. It became clear that real kinship is more about commitment than biology. The effort it took to adopt David produced a stronger bond than if we had had a child easily, taken it for granted, or focused on its demands rather than its joys. This gave me an enduring realization that this child, any child, is a gift to be enjoyed, not a burden to be accepted. The joys and realities of parenthood took precedence and the struggle of infertility receded. While adoption might not be everyone's solution, I found it grace-filled and satisfying.

But my family situation was not a happily-ever-after one. Two years later, I found myself the single parent of a toddler. I never lost my delight at being David's mother, but now the same-faith partnership and intact family that I had envisioned were even further from my reach. I wondered if I even had the right to use the word "family" in connection with my current situation.

Church again became a hard place to be as I focused again on children sitting with parents, siblings, and grandparents. It felt like my son and I, two biologically unrelated people brought together by God and love, were cast adrift in a strange place. We had neither relatives nor roots where my job was. Connections to everything and everyone had to be done intentionally and with effort. It was very difficult and lonely. On my own I might have just succumbed to despair, but I couldn't do that to this sweet little boy whom I loved so much. For his sake I tried hard to cobble together a semblance of family. In more ways than one, this adoptive bond that grace had brought to me, and which effort and time had forged strong, was life saving.

CHURCH

The New Testament principle that we are all adopted into God's family now took on more meaning.[2] No one has a privileged place in God's eyes. All of us are equal and all of us are chosen. Those of us who have been in the church longer should not lord it over others, creating an "insider" versus "outsider" situation. Instead, we should seek to share this good news ("gospel") and invite others into the household of God. After all, the Greek word for church, *ecclesia*, means those who are "called forth." We are all called into relationship by God.

God gives us the church to be our shelter and family. Occasionally the church functioned this way for us, especially within the seminary community where I was teaching. But what we missed was a sense of connection that felt more ongoing and daily. I often wished that some grandparents, aunts and uncles, or sisters and brothers in the church could adopt us. But it seemed the local church didn't have many natural connections for a divorced, highly educated, and ordained single mother and her child. There were affinity groups or classes for children, married couples, retired folk, young singles, but little for the loose ends of society's families.

Now it became clear that the church is not simply neutral or inadequate in the midst of social change. If the church does not intentionally welcome and find a place for strangers and those without natural ties, it adds to the societal alienation. All of us were once strangers to God and slaves to other things. But now, we learn in scripture, we have received adoption as sons and daughters of God (Gal. 3:26–4:8). That means we are all family to each other, whether we are biologically related or not. The biblical mandate is one of including the outcasts and strangers, not just biological family members.

Of course, today in our increasingly mobile and individualistic society, nuclear families need the help a church can give. But are we creating other problems with our stress on maintaining strong family ties? While once I wanted nothing more than my own family at church, now I looked around and saw the inadequacy of this goal.[3] I began to ask myself: How many people in these pews really live in "the perfect Christian family"? How many cry silently through the Mother's or Father's Day services because of infertility, miscarriage, divorce, or death? How many feel empty because they have no one to send to Sunday school, confirmation, or youth group? How many potential friendships do people miss because they think they must fit into the existing groups that do not fit them? How many folk simply stay away from church altogether because of these factors? I realized much more clearly now how outsiders are not just excluded, but created.

Too often in the church, human affiliation becomes a "do-it-yourself" project requiring constant effort. For those without natural bonds, it is even more difficult, akin to building with very few tools. The unconnected ones can seem like a burden, an embarrassment, or a reminder of the fragility of human connection, for their presence makes it frighteningly clear to the others that it is ultimately futile to base one's security upon biological connections.

The Bible is full of stories of widows and orphans, foreigners, strangers and sojourners, people disconnected from family and roots. The scriptural narrative often shows how they become connected with others in unexpected ways, as well as admonishing us not to neglect others like them. Although the Hebrew people are admonished not to marry foreigners, since they might then be led away from their God (Ezra 10:2; Prov. 5:20), they also are commanded to extend kindness to strangers, since they were once strangers and sojourners themselves (Exod. 20:10, 22:21, 23:9). After all, the Hebrew people had been pushed out of one land and sent into exile, had wandered and been persecuted. They knew very well what it was like to be strangers, cut off from their land and their natural ties (Ps. 137:4; Exod. 2:22, 18:3).

There are also instances when the Hebrew people were instructed to welcome the stranger because in so doing they may be entertaining God. In Genesis 18, when Abraham and Sarah welcome and feed the three visitors, they find out later that they are actually divine emissaries. The vision of being a people of God makes it imperative to include the stranger. The biblical mandate is one of inclusion.

The story of Ruth and Naomi is a model that brings together these elements. Elimelech, his wife Naomi, and their two sons move from Bethlehem in Judah to the foreign land of Moab. These sons take Moabite wives and all goes well until the three men die. At this point, Naomi implores her two daughters-in-law to go back to their biological kin, for there they might have a hope of survival. One goes back, but the other, Ruth, loves her mother-in-law so much that she insists, "Do not press me to leave you or to turn back from following you! Where you go, I will go; where you lodge, I will lodge; your people shall be my people, and your God my God" (Ruth 1:16).

Ruth had come to know and love this foreign family and foreign God. Naomi, who knew both what it felt like to be a stranger and how to welcome a stranger into her home, saw before her the value of the kinship bond that depended on a relational covenant rather than a biological tie. Naomi and Ruth go back to the land of Judah and through Ruth's devotion a new family is formed that ensures the survival of all. The women friends of Naomi affirm this by saying, "your daughter-in-law who loves you . . . is more to you than seven sons" (Ruth 4:15).

The New Testament continues the theme of openness to foreigners, strangers, or sojourners. It is again suggested that by providing for the stranger, we might be entertaining God without realizing it (Matt. 25:35–40). The New Testament continues to urge us to show hospitality to strangers (Heb. 13:2). And if through our love they experience God's grace, and recognize God's voice, they will be strangers no longer (Eph. 2:19).

Today, many people feel isolated and detached. Yet Jesus said he would not leave us orphaned. The church, the people of God, is a place where people are promised welcome and hospitality. At its best, it is a glimmer of divine inclusion, a covenant with an eternal partner who has the persistent habit of binding us to others. At its best, it is graced with the Spirit's presence and connecting power.

This kind of kinship is not based on biology, role, or function, but simply on the recognition that the same God claims us. Similar to the blood connection about which you have no choice, the church connection is recognition of a permanent kinship through God. It recognizes that all of us who hear God's voice in

Christ are related to one another. We have all been adopted, and God has made a great effort to forge that bond. It was God who took the initiative and ultimately it is God, not us, who sustains it. But, again like a biological family, a strong measure of human intentionality and commitment is essential. Without our recognition of the bond and appropriate actions to go with it, the connection is thin and lifeless. But none of us automatically knows how this should work. Being a part of the church is a learning process as we are formed through word, sacrament, and the Spirit's guidance, to become like Christ and to help with the uniting work of God. In fact, in the church we learn to be family, not only to each other, but also to the whole world.

Such a vision of the church should lead to a local congregation structured as a network of smaller communities, each of which stays aware of its members. Then mutual help can be provided in dignified and compassionate ways. A core of older persons with no grandchildren or with families far away may be delighted to team together and help as surrogate grandparents. Handy persons who find their delight in home or car maintenance can offer services and instruction. A teenage boy might value a role model outside his nuclear family and have some nascent babysitting skills. A retired woman at home still has love and skills to give.

Many times I have been graced by such communal caretaking. During a crisis, my colleagues helped me gather my belongings, and the dean took us into his own home for a time. Through David's younger years, my students often babysat so I could have a free night or attend to business. When my father died, I was taken aback by all the condolences I received from my seminary community, even though I was away on sabbatical. When I finally decided to buy a house, a dozen students offered their aid. When I was overwhelmed by the inevitable problems of home ownership, a retired clergy colleague used his considerable expertise to help with repairs.

But there is more the church can do. Liturgies and services could creatively address infertility, divorce, single parenting, or other challenges, but also celebrate accomplishments as any healthy family would. An ethos of abundance and welcome is more in keeping with gospel promises. The church is the advance guard of God's new creation inaugurated in Jesus Christ, not a waiting room filled with despairing or passive patients.

Sometimes I still wish I could live in a vibrant extended family, with lots of children, a partner, and many relations and friends living close together. It seems simpler that way. But the deeper grace I've experienced did not come through this route. The combination of my interfaith background, infertility, and spiritual journey has caused my initial hopes and expectations to change considerably. Now I know that kinship and relationship is not as much about biological connections as about commitment. I now realize that God's calling is not epitomized in creating one's own family or in securing one's insider status, whether to ethnic group, religion, race, or culture. Instead, God's way works through the intentional bonds of belief and the inclusion of the outsider that is possible in the church. And, most of all, I see that the biological family reveals only a fragile glimmer of the rich interconnectedness that God intends for all of us.

Scripture and tradition give us various images of the church—people, body, communion, and Spirit—which should help us envision the church in a larger, deeper way than simply as institution.[4] We are the people of God, called forth from throughout the world. Ethnic, national, and biological ties are put aside. We make up a new people, the "body of Christ." We have a new identity as a community created by Christ's work and sacrifice. We are a fellowship that models interpersonal love and fulfilling relationship, where we each look out for our neighbor's welfare. All of this is empowered by the Spirit's love and creativity. The Spirit lives inside each of us and in the community as a whole.

Our communion is not just of our own efforts, but is the Spirit's work and energy.

These lessons have required different things from me than I expected when I set out to forge together my faith and family. But no one ever knows where the path will lead when they begin to walk. The road to Emmaus leads to the surprise of Christ's presence. There the encounter and conversation with the stranger leads to a shared meal around the table with people with whom we least expect it. And those shared meals begin to forge the bonds that are the backbone of the church.

ENDNOTES

INTRODUCTION: Longing

1. Laurie Lisle, *Without Child: Challenging the Stigma of Childlessness* (New York: Ballantine Books, 1996), 42; on the status of the social mother in America, see Lisle's discussion on pages 72–74, 107–08, 184–85. See also Helena Michie and Naomi R. Cahn, *Confinements: Fertility and Infertility in Contemporary Culture* (New Brunswick, NJ: Rutgers University Press, 1997), on childlessness in America.

2. On American pronatalist and promaternal efforts, see Elaine Tyler May, *Barren in the Promised Land: Childless Americans and the Pursuit of Happiness* (Cambridge, MA: Harvard University Press, 1997). Tyler May discusses the race suicide panic in chapter 2 of *Barren in the Promised Land.*

Recent feminist works document how our culture valorizes Euro-American motherhood while denigrating that of African American women and Latinas. See for example, Dorothy E. Roberts, *Killing the Black Body: Race, Reproduction, and the Meaning of Liberty* (New York:

Pantheon Books, 1997) and Patricia Hill Collins, "A Comparison of Two Works on Black Family Life," *Signs* 15, no. 4 (Summer 1989): 875–84.

3. Tyler May, *Barren,* 17–19.

4. Patricia Irwin Johnson, *Adopting After Infertility* (Indianapolis: Perspectives Press, 1992), 20.

5. On reproductive loss and technology see Lisa Cartwright, *Screening the Body* (Minneapolis: University of Minnesota Press, 1985). A piggy-back phenomenon of the rise of ART is the increased use of home pregnancy tests. It is now possible to detect pregnancy within days of conception—one woman went on a shopping spree at a children's clothing store because "the stick turned pink this morning!" One unintended result of this home health care is the rise in known numbers of very early miscarriages. Biological studies estimate that 50 percent of conceptions end in miscarriage during the initial two weeks of pregnancy. While prior generations would never have known or even possibly suspected such miscarriages, contemporary women can date them.

6. Elizabeth Barthelot, *Family Bonds: Adoption and the Politics of Parenthood* (Boston: Houghton Mifflin, 1993), 35.

7. On the corrosive effects of infertility on women's sense of self, see Mardy S. Ireland, *Reconceiving Women: Separating Motherhood from Female Identity* (New York: Guilford Press, 1993); Nancy Gieseler Devor, "Pastoral Care for Infertile Couples," *The Journal of Pastoral Care* 48, no. 4 (Winter 1994): 355–60; Beth Spring, "Ministry to the Infertile," *Leadership* 9 (Summer 1988): 95–97; and "When the Dream Child Dies," *Christianity Today,* 31: 27–31.

8. For general discussions of the social construction of reproductive loss see Gayle Letherby, "The Meaning of Miscarriage," *Women's Studies International Forum* 16, no. 2 (1993): 165–80; Linda L. Layne, "Motherhood Lost: Cultural Dimensions of Miscarriage and Stillbirth in America," *Women & Health* 16, no. 3/4 (1990): 69–98; Helen Hardacre, *Marketing the Menacing Fetus* (Berkeley: University of California Press, 1997); and Sarah Matthews and Laura Wexler, *Pregnant Pictures* (New York: Routledge, 2000).

9. Maggie Kirkman, "Infertile Women and the Narrative Work of Mourning," *Narrative Inquiry* 13, no. 1 (2003): 244. Kirkman argues that part of the grief work in relation to infertility can be understood as revising the autobiographical narrative in order to accommodate infertility's disruption to the plot of one's life.

In *Taking Charge of Infertility* (Indianapolis: Perspectives Press, 1994), Patricia Irwin Johnson identifies six potential losses of infertility: loss of control; loss of individual genetic continuity; loss of a jointly conceived child; loss of the physical expectations surrounding pregnancy and the power to impregnate; loss of the emotional expectations regarding pregnancy, birth, and breastfeeding; and the loss of the opportunity to parent.

10. Discussions of theology as the mediator between the Christian tradition and common human experience can be found in David Tracy, *Blessed Rage for Order: The New Pluralism in Theology* (New York: Seabury Press, 1975) and *The Analogical Imagination: Christian Theology and the Culture of Pluralism* (New York: Crossroads, 1981). See also Gordon Kaufman, *An Essay on Theological Method* (Missoula, MO: Scholars Press for the American Academy of Religion, 1975) and *In Face of Mystery: A Constructive Theology* (Cambridge, MA: Harvard University Press, 1993), on the imaginative and constructive nature of theology. Feminist theology places particular emphasis on the critical role of human experience in theological understanding; see Anne Carr, *Transforming Grace: Christian Tradition and Women's Experience* (New York: Continuum, 1996); Rosemary Radford Ruether, *Women and Redemption: A Theological History* (Minneapolis: Augsburg Fortress Press, 1998); and Ann O'Hara Graff, ed., *In the Embrace of God: Feminist Approaches to Theological Anthropology* (Maryknoll, NY: Orbis Books, 1995).

Philosophical works supporting the role of experience in knowledge include Elizabeth Kamarck Minnich, *Transforming Knowledge* (Philadelphia: Temple University Press, 1990), and Mark Johnson, *The Body in the Mind: The Bodily Basis of Meaning, Imagination, and Reason* (Chicago: University of Chicago, 1987).

ONE: Why

1. The question of how a powerful and loving God allows the presence of suffering and evil in the world is the classical problem of *theodicy*. Among the books that helpfully address this question is Tyron Inbody's *The Transforming God: An Interpretation of Suffering and Evil* (Louisville, KY: Westminster John Knox Press, 1997). Inbody argues that classical theism often trivializes the reality of evil in order to affirm a God who is both powerful and loving and proposes that God's power

must be reconceptualized in order to uphold both a loving God and the reality of evil in this world. Jewish Scripture scholar Jon Levenson promotes a theodicy of God's ongoing struggle against evil in *Creation and the Persistence of Evil: The Jewish Drama of Divine Omnipotence* (San Francisco: Harper & Row, 1988).

An earlier article of mine that works with issues of infertility and God's providence is entitled "Re-Imagining God's Providence," *Brethren Life and Thought* 44, no. 3 (Summer 1999): 7–21.

2. For Calvin on the providence of God see *Institutes of the Christian Religion,* vol. I, sections xvi–xviii. Current surveys of the concept are available in various theological dictionaries such as *Evangelical Dictionary of Theology,* ed. Walter A. Elwell (Grand Rapids, MI: Baker Book House, 1984), and *The Westminster Dictionary of Christian Theology,* ed. Alan Richardson and John Bowden (Philadelphia: Westminster Press, 1983).

3. Several books offer constructive work on a Christian theology of suffering. Among the most helpful are Douglas John Hall, *God and Human Suffering: An Exercise in the Theology of the Cross* (Minneapolis: Augsburg Publishing, 1986); J. Christiaan Beker, *Suffering and Hope: The Biblical Vision and the Human Predicament* (Philadelphia: Fortress Press, 1987); and Stanley Hauerwas, *God, Medicine, and Suffering* (Grand Rapids, MI: Wm. B. Eerdmans, reprint, 2000).

4. Peter Berger describes the state in which we no longer have but are our emotions in *Redeeming Laughter: The Comic Dimension of Human Experience* (New York: Walter de Gruyter, 1997), 47.

5. The experience of bereavement and the shock to the self-identity of the surviving loved ones is described by Todd DuBose in "The Phenomenology of Bereavement, Grief, and Mourning," *Journal of Religion and Health* 36, no. 4 (Winter 1997): 367–74. This sense of loss reverberates in Raymond A. Anselment's study of the poetry and meditations that have been occasioned by miscarriage from the seventeenth century to the present day ("'A Heart Terrifying Sorrow': An Occasional Piece on Poetry of Miscarriage," *Papers on Language & Literature* 33, no. 1 [Winter 1997]: 13–46).

With the growth of the Internet, Web sites designed by parents who have experienced loss through miscarriage, stillbirth, or the death of a child now abound. Many sites are a tribute or memorial for their lost loved one.

6. Two powerful collections of contemporary laments are Ann Weems' *Psalms of Lament* (Louisville, KY: Westminster John Knox Press, 1995) and Nicholas Wolterstorff's *Lament for a Son* (Grand Rapids, MI: Wm B. Eerdmans, 1987). Both were written in response to the deaths of young adult sons.

7. Sallie McFague, *The Body of God: An Ecological Theology* (Minneapolis: Augsburg Fortress Press, 1993), vii. In this book and her prior volume, *Models of God: Theology for an Ecological, Nuclear Age* (Philadelphia: Fortress Press, 1987), McFague argues for a concept of God that takes more seriously the incarnational aspects of God's work with humanity and re-imagines "the world as God's Body."

8. The question of how theologians do justice to the "messiness and tragedy of dying" is asked poignantly by Paula Cooey in her editorial entitled, "The Messiness of Dying," *Journal of Feminist Studies in Religion* 15, no. 1 (Spring 1999): 96–98. She echoes the conviction expressed in our "Introduction" that theological work be more honest in addressing the reality and tragedy of many life situations.

TWO: Sorrow

1. It has become commonplace to remind Christian churches that Mother's Day is not a holy day. Sometimes the flip remark is added, "It's a Hallmark holiday." This is not quite true either. Instituted by Congress in 1914, the American celebration of Mother's Day has a disturbing history. With roots in mid-nineteenth century anti-immigrant and racist fears, Mother's Day was intended to stir dreams of babies among the white, educated American women whom Congress feared were being "outbred" by their poorer and darker sisters. See Elaine Tyler May, *Barren in the Promised Land: Childless Americans and the Pursuit of Happiness* (Cambridge, MA: Harvard University Press, 1997), 64.

2. There is abundant literature on the Barren Matriarch narratives. Scholars differ in the particulars of their interpretations of the primary theological function of these stories, but agree that they are not so much about difficulty conceiving (which is our preoccupation) but with the implementation of God's salvific will broadly understood. Some argue that the matriarchs are a personified Israel and the narratives of their long-delayed conceptions and eventual pregnancies demonstrate God's sovereignty over Israel (Blessing) or the fragility of "the chain of the

covenant" (Dresner). Others argue that they serve to illustrate God's transcendence over life and death (Ackerman). These are theological narratives, not clinical case studies. Their overarching concern is to reveal who God is and what God wants for us. See Kamila Blessing, "Desolate Jerusalem and Barren Matriarch: Two Distinct Figures in the Pseudepigrapha," *Journal for the Study of the Pseudepigrapha* 18 (October 1998): 47–69; Samuel H. Dresner, "Barren Rachel," *Judaism* 40 (Fall 1991): 442–51; Susan Ackerman, "Child Sacrifice: Returning God's Gift," *Bible Review* 9 (June 1993): 20–28, 56.

3. In *Taking Charge of Infertility* (Indianapolis: Perspectives Press, 1994), Patricia Irwin Johnson writes of how personal resources are taxed by infertility. See, for example, pages 71–73.

4. Paul Tillich, *Dynamics of Faith* (New York: Harper & Row, 1957). See in particular chapter 1. For an analysis of Tillich's thought and his concept of ultimate concern, see Langdon Gilkey, *Gilkey on Tillich* (New York: Crossroad, 1990).

5. Elizabeth Barthelot, *Family Bonds: Adoption and the Politics of Parenthood* (Boston: Houghton Mifflin, 1993). See also *Families by Law: An Adoption Reader,* ed. Naomi R. Cahn and Joan Heifetz Hollinger (New York: New York University Press, 2004).

6. These observations from a waiting room come from Jill Bialosky and Helen Schulman, eds., *Wanting a Child: Twenty-Two Writers on Their Difficult but Mostly Successful Quests for Parenthood in a High-Tech Age* (New York: Farrar, Straus and Giroux, 1998), 4.

7. W. Herbst, s.v. "Envy," *The New Catholic Encyclopedia,* 2nd ed., 2003.

8. W. Gerrod Parrott, "The Emotional Experiences of Envy and Jealousy," in *The Psychology of Jealousy and Envy,* ed. Peter Slovey (New York: Guilford Press, 1991), 3–30.

9. There are many translations of Thomas's *Summa* available. The version used in this essay is the translation by the Fathers of the English Dominican Provinces, *Summa Theologica* (Westminster, MD: Christian Classics, 1981). Thomas's consideration of envy is found in IIa, IIae, Q. 36. On mortal sin, see IIa, IIae, Q. 25, art. 3.

10. On Thomas's account of the passions, see Richard R. Baker, *The Thomistic Theory of the Passions and Their Influence upon the Will* (Notre Dame, IN: University of Notre Dame, 1941), and G. Simon

Harak, *Virtuous Passions: The Formation of Christian Character* (New York: Paulist Press, 1993).

11. Karl Rahner, "Reflections on the Unity of the Love of Neighbor and the Love of God," *Theological Investigations: Concerning Vatican II*, vol. VI, trans. Karl H. and Boniface Kruger (New York: Crossroad, 1982), 231–49. For an introduction to Rahner's thought, see Leo O'Donovon, ed., *A World of Grace* (New York: Crossroad, 1984). James F. Bresnahan's essay "An Ethics of Faith" (chap. 12) is of particular interest on this point.

12. Márta Guóth-Gumberger, "Buried Under a Mango Tree: Infertility and Faith," *Daughters of Sarah* 18, no. 4 (Fall 1992), 12; emphasis in the original.

13. *On the Dignity and Vocation of Women (Mulieris Dignitatem)* was issued in 1998 by Pope John Paul II. An English translation is available in *Origins* 18/17 (6 October 1998): 261–83. For a sample of feminist reaction and analysis, see Lisa Sowle Cahill, *Family: A Christian Social Perspective* (Minneapolis: Augsburg Fortress Press, 2000), 92, and Susan A. Ross, *Extravagant Affections: A Feminist Sacramental Theology* (New York: Continuum, 1998), 107–15.

14. Wendell Berry, *A Timbered Choir: The Sabbath Poems, 1979-1997* (Washington, D.C.: Counterpoint, 1998), 1994: Poem III.

15. Pierre Teilhard de Chardin, "The Mass on the World," *The Heart of Matter*, trans. René Hague (San Diego: Harcourt Brace Jovanovich, 1978), 119–34. For a brief discussion of the section quoted in this chapter, see Thomas M. King, *Teilhard's Mysticism of Knowing* (New York: Seabury Press, 1981), 142–48.

THREE: Rupture

1. Therese A. Rando, *Treatment of Complicated Mourning* (Champaign, IL: Research Press, 1993), provides a clinical description of grief occasioned by reproductive loss.

2. A compelling account of the interplay between powerlessness and guilt is given in Beth Powning's *Shadow Child: An Apprenticeship in Love and Loss* (New York: Carroll and Graf Publishers, 1999).

3. Jürgen Moltmann's *The Crucified God: The Cross of Christ as the Foundation and the Criticism of Christian Theology* (San Francisco: Harper & Row, 1973) is indispensable reading on the claim that God

takes death into Godself. Karl Barth is Moltmann's forerunner in reinvigorating the doctrine of the Trinity for contemporary believers. An influential recent work on the Trinity is Catherine Mowry LaCugna's *God for Us: The Trinity and Christian Life* (San Francisco: HarperSanFrancisco, 1993).

In an earlier version of this chapter I was more explicit about these theological links (*Modern Theology* 17:2 [April 2001]: 227–45).

4. For further reading on ritual and women's experience, see Charlotte Caron, *To Make and Make Again: Feminist Ritual Thealogy* (New York: Crossroad, 1993); Wendy Hunter Roberts, *Celebrating Her: Feminist Ritualizing Comes of Age* (Cleveland: Pilgrim Press, 1998); Lesley A. Northup, *Ritualizing Women: Patterns of Spirituality* (Cleveland: Pilgrim Press, 1997); and the books edited by Miriam Therese Winter, *WomanWord* (New York: Crossroad, 1990), *WomanWisdom* (New York: Crossroad, 1991), and *WomanWitness* (New York: Crossroad, 1992).

FOUR: Comfort

1. The literature on quickening has helped me understand medieval tripartite anthropology whereby each human person was understood to be constituted by body, spirit, and soul. Along this research path, I also learned an interesting fact of etymology. The word "quick" has its etymological roots in an Old Norse term for life. "Quick" here does not refer to speed; instead it refers to one's life principle or life source. It is akin to our use of the term "heart" to mark what is central to one's self. We have retained this sense of "quick" as fundamental life or soul in our expression: "it cuts me to the quick."

Exploring features of sixteenth-century understandings of pregnancy as quickening demonstrates the ways that reproductive practices and beliefs shape our perspectives on human procreation. The phrase "history of reproduction" initially may sound odd to our ears. We usually think of pregnancy as a biological condition, not a social institution; and we do not think of reproduction as having a history. Yet historians help us see how our contemporary understandings of pregnancy and pregnancy loss are shaped by modern medical practices and modern understandings of embryology.

2. Pastors and chaplains have developed an array of rituals and prayers for miscarriage and stillbirth. See, for example, Bertha Landers,

Through Laughter and Tears—The Church Celebrates: Rites of Passage and Pilgrimage in the Christian Church (Scottsdale, PA: Mennonite Publishing House, 2001); and Carol M. Norén, *In Time of Crisis and Sorrow: A Minister's Manual Resource Guide* (San Francisco: Jossey-Bass, 2001). Some denominations have also begun including such rituals and prayers in their books of worship such as *The United Methodist Book of Worship* (Nashville, TN: United Methodist Publishing House, 1992); *Book of Blessings,* National Conference of Catholic Bishops (Collegeville, MN: Liturgical Press, 1989); *Occasional Services: A Companion to the Lutheran Book of Worship* (Minneapolis: Augsburg Publishing House, 1982); *Book of Common Worship,* Presbyterian Church (Louisville, KY: Westminster John Knox Press, 1993); and for the Episcopal Church, Elizabeth Rankin Geitz, Marjorie A. Burke, and Ann Smith, eds., *Women's Uncommon Prayers: Our Lives Revealed, Nurtured, Celebrated* (Harrisburg, PA: Morehouse Publishing, 2000).

3. An English translation of Luther's 1529 Large Catechism can be found in *The Book of Concord: The Confessions of the Evangelical Lutheran Church,* edited and translated by Theodore G. Tappert, Jaroslav Pelikan, Robert H. Fischer, and Arthur C. Piepkorn (Philadelphia: Fortress Press, 1959), 357–461.

4. On women in the medieval period, see Joan Cadden, *Meanings of Sex Difference in the Middle Ages: Medicine, Science and Culture,* Cambridge History of Medicine series (Cambridge: Cambridge University Press, 1993), 233. On baptism Cadden cites John Douglas Close Fisher, *Christian Initiation: Baptism in the Medieval West, a Study in the Disintegration of the Primitive Rite of Initiation* (London: SPCK, 1965), 110–12. On the sense of urgency around baptism at this time, see Susan C. Karant-Nunn, *The Reformation of Ritual: An Interpretation of Early Modern Germany,* Christianity and Society in the Modern World series (London and New York: Routledge, 1997). Karant-Nunn comments, "So great were the protective virtues ascribed to baptism that parents were unwilling to risk postponing the ritual" (p. 44).

5. The remarks on Zwingli and infant baptism can be found in volume 5 of the *New Schaff-Herzog Encyclopedia of Religious Knowledge,* 490; for Luther see page 491.

6. Jane E. Strohl's translation of Luther's letter on his daughter's death can be found in Strohl's essay, "The Child in Luther's Theology:

'For What Purpose Do We Older Folks Exist Other Than to Care for . . . the Young?'" in *The Child in Christian Thought,* ed. Marcia J. Bunge (Grand Rapids, MI: Wm B. Eerdmans, 2001), 157.

FIVE: Faith

1. *The Baltimore Catechism,* Lesson 10, Question 109.

2. Jeanne Stevenson-Moessner, in *The Spirit of Adoption: At Home in God's Family* (Louisville, KY: Westminster John Knox Press, 2003), offers an extended theological analysis of the metaphor of adoption in the New Testament and argues for its value in contemporary ecclesiological discussion. See also *Family: A Christian Social Perspective* by Lisa Sowle Cahill (Minneapolis: Augsburg Fortress Press, 2000) for historical and theological analyses of the concept of family.

3. Concerning our unrealistic expectations of family, especially in light of Christian teaching, see Janet Fishburn, *Confronting the Idolatry of Family: A New Vision for the Household of God* (Nashville: Abingdon Press, 1991). For a historical perspective on how some of our expectations about family expectations are more contextual than spiritual, see Rosemary Radford Ruether, *Christianity and the Making of the Modern Family* (Boston: Beacon Press, 2000).

4. For further reading on theologies of the church, see Letty Russell, *Church in the Round: Feminist Interpretation of the Church* (Louisville, KY: Westminster John Knox Press, 1993) and Robert Kysar, *Stumbling in the Light: New Testament Images for a Changing Church* (St. Louis, MO: Chalice Press, 1999).

BIBLIOGRAPHY

Reproductive Loss: Infertility, Miscarriage, and Stillbirth

Berg, Barbara J. *Nothing to Cry About*. New York: Putnam Publishing Group, 1981.

Bialosky, Jill, and Helen Schulman, eds. *Wanting a Child: Twenty-Two Writers on Their Difficult but Mostly Successful Quests for Parenthood in a High-Tech Age*. New York: Farrar, Straus and Giroux, 1998.

Borg, Susan, and Judith N. Lasker. *In Search of Parenthood: Coping with Infertility and Hi-Tech Conception*. Boston: Beacon Press, 1987.

_____ . *When Pregnancy Fails: Families Coping with Miscarriage, Ectopic Pregnancy, Stillbirth, and Infant Death*. New York: Bantam Books, 1989.

Carr, Bobbi. "Neither Sound nor Sight." *Yale Journal of Law and Feminism* 16, no. 4 (Fall 1990): 153–59.

Cooper, Susan Lewis, and Ellen Sarasohn Glazer. *Choosing Assisted Reproduction: Social, Emotional, and Ethical Considerations*. Indianapolis: Perspectives Press, 1998.

Davis, Deborah. *Empty Cradle, Broken Heart: Surviving the Death of Your Baby.* Rev. ed. Golden, CO: Fulcrum Publishing, 1996.

Friedman, Rochelle, and Bonnie Gradstein. *Surviving Pregnancy Loss.* Boston: Little, Brown, 1982.

Gilbert, Kathleen R., and Laura S. Smart. *Coping with Infant or Fetal Loss: The Couple's Healing Process.* New York: Brunner, 1992.

Glazer, Ellen Sarasohn. *Without Child: Experiencing and Resolving Infertility.* Lexington, MA: Lexington Books, 1988.

Greil, Larry L., and Arthur L. Greil. *Not Yet Pregnant: Infertile Couples in Contemporary America.* New Brunswick, NJ: Rutgers University Press, 1991.

Hanson, Melissa Sexson. *When Mourning Breaks: Coping with Miscarriage.* Harrisburg, PA: Morehouse Publishing, 1998.

Harkness, Carla. *The Infertility Book: A Comprehensive Medical & Emotional Guide.* Berkeley: Celestial Arts, 1992.

Ilse, Sherokee. *Empty Arms: Coping after Miscarriage, Stillbirth, and Infant Death.* Rev. ed., Maple Plain, MN: Wintergreen Press, 2000.

Johnson, Patricia Irwin. *Taking Charge of Infertility.* Indianapolis: Perspectives Press, 1994.

Knapp, Ronald J. *Beyond Endurance: When a Child Dies.* New York: Schocken Books, 1986.

Kohn, Ingrid, and Perry-Lynn Moffitt. *A Silent Sorrow: Pregnancy Loss—Guidance and Support for You and Your Family.* 2nd ed. New York: Routledge, 2000.

Lafser, Christine O'Keeffe. *An Empty Cradle, a Full Heart: Reflections for Mothers and Fathers After Miscarriage, Stillbirth, or Infant Death.* Chicago: Loyola Press, 1998.

Layne, Linda L. "Breaking the Silence: An Agenda for a Feminist Discourse of Pregnancy Loss." *Feminist Studies* 23, no. 2 (Summer 1997): 289–315.

Lublin, Nancy. *Pandora's Box: Feminism Confronts Reproductive Technology.* Lanham, MD: Rowman & Littlefield Publishers, 1998.

McGuirk, James, and Mary Elizabeth McGuirk. *For Want of Child.* New York: Continuum, 1991.

Michie, Helena, and Naomi R. Cahn, eds. *Confinements: Fertility and Infertility in Contemporary Culture.* New Brunswick, NJ: Rutgers University Press, 1996.

Monach, James H. *Childless, No Choice: The Experience of Involuntary Childlessness.* New York: Routledge, 1993.

Mullens, Anne. *Missed Conceptions: Overcoming Infertility.* Toronto: McGraw-Hill Ryerson, 1990.

Nachtigall, Robert, and Elizabeth Mehren. *Overcoming Infertility.* New York: Doubleday, 1991.

Parkes, Colin Murray, Pittu Laungani, and Bill Young, eds. *Death and Bereavement Across Cultures.* New York: Routledge, 1997.

Pizer, Hank, and Christine O'Brien Palinski. *Coping with Miscarriage.* New York: Dial, 1980.

Powning, Beth. *Shadow Child: An Apprenticeship in Love and Loss.* New York: Carroll and Graf Publishers, 1999.

Rue, Nancy. *Handling the Heartbreak of Miscarriage.* San Bernadino, CA: Here's Life Publications, 1987.

Salzer, Linda P. *Surviving Infertility: A Compassionate Guide through the Emotional Crisis of Infertility.* New York: HarperPerennial, 1991.

Sandelowski, Margarete. *With Child in Mind: Studies of the Personal Encounter with Infertility.* Philadelphia: University of Pennsylvania, 1993.

Schwiebert, Pat, and Paul Kirk. *When Hello Means Goodbye: A Guide for Parents Whose Child Dies before Birth, at Birth or Shortly after Birth.* Portland, OR: Perinatal Loss, 1985.

Stephenson, Lynda. *Give Us a Child: Coping with the Personal Crisis of Infertility.* Grand Rapids, MI: Zondervan, 1992.

Stigger, Judith A. *Coping with Infertility.* Minneapolis: Augsburg Publishing House, 1983.

Stout, Martha. *Without Child: A Compassionate Look at Infertility.* Grand Rapids, MI: Zondervan, 1985.

Vredevelt, Pam W. *Empty Arms: Hope and Support for Those Who Have Suffered a Miscarriage, Stillbirth, or Tubal Pregnancy.* Rev. ed. Portland, OR: Multnomah Press, 2001.

Society and Motherhood

Barthelot, Elizabeth. *Family Bonds: Adoption and the Politics of Parenthood.* Boston: Houghton Mifflin, 1993.

Cahill, Lisa Sowle. *Family: A Christian Social Perspective.* Minneapolis: Augsburg Fortress Press, 2000.

Hansen, Elaine Tuttle. *Mother Without Child: Contemporary Fiction and the Crisis of Motherhood.* Berkeley: University of California Press, 1997.

Hardacre, Helen. *Marketing the Menacing Fetus.* Berkeley: University of California Press, 1997.

Hays, Sharon. *The Cultural Contradictions of Motherhood.* New Haven, CT: Yale University Press, 1996.

Ireland, Mardy S. *Reconceiving Women: Separating Motherhood from Female Identity.* New York: Guilford Press, 1993.

Johnson, Patricia Irwin. *Adopting after Infertility.* Indianapolis: Perspectives Press, 1992.

Kaplan, E. Ann. *Motherhood and Representation: The Mother in Popular Culture and Melodrama.* New York: Routledge, 1992.

Layne, Linda L. "Motherhood Lost: Cultural Dimensions of Miscarriage and Stillbirth in America." *Women & Health* 16, no. 3/4 (1990): 69–98.

Letherby, Gayle. "The Meaning of Miscarriage." *Women's Studies International Forum* 16, no. 2 (1993): 165–80.

Lisle, Laurie. *Without Child: Challenging the Stigma of Childlessness.* New York: Ballantine Books, 1996.

Marsh, Margaret, and Wanda Ronner. *The Empty Cradle: Infertility in America from Colonial Times to the Present.* Baltimore: The Johns Hopkins University Press, 1996.

Matthews, Sarah, and Laura Wexler. *Pregnant Pictures.* New York: Routledge, 2000.

May, Elaine Tyler. *Barren in the Promised Land: Childless Americans and the Pursuit of Happiness.* Cambridge, MA: Harvard University Press, 1997.

Michie, Helena, and Naomi R. Cahn. *Confinements: Fertility and Infertility in Contemporary Culture.* New Brunswick, NJ: Rutgers University Press, 1997.

Roberts, Dorothy E. *Killing the Black Body: Race, Reproduction, and the Meaning of Liberty.* New York: Pantheon Books, 1997.

Sandelowski, Margarete J. "Failures of Volition: Female Agency and Infertility in Historical Perspective." *Signs* 15, no. 3 (Spring 1990): 475–99.

Shulgold, Barbara, and Lynne Sipiora. *Dear Barbara, Dear Lynne: The True Story of Two Women in Search of Motherhood.* Reading, MA: Addison-Wesley Publishing, 1992.

Theological Resources

Adams, Marilyn McCord. *Horrendous Evils and the Goodness of God.* Ithaca: Cornell University Press, 1999.

Beker, J. Christiaan. *Suffering and Hope: The Biblical Vision and the Human Predicament.* Philadelphia: Fortress Press, 1987.

Cooey, Paula M. "The Messiness of Dying." *Journal of Feminist Studies in Religion* 15, no. 1 (Spring 1999): 96–98.

Fishburn, Janet. *Confronting the Idolatry of Family: A New Vision for the Household of God.* Nashville: Abingdon Press, 1991.

Frantz, Nadine Pence. "Re-Imagining God's Providence." *Brethren Life and Thought* 44, no. 3 (Summer 1999): 7–21.

Hall, Douglas John. *God and Human Suffering: An Exercise in the Theology of the Cross.* Minneapolis: Augsburg Publishing, 1986.

Harrison, Beverly W., ed. Special Issue: "Rhetorics, Rituals and Conflicts Over Women's Reproductive Power." *Journal of Feminist Studies in Religion* 11, no. 2 (Fall 1995): 1–4.

Hauerwas, Stanley, ed. *God, Medicine, and Suffering.* Grand Rapids, MI: Wm. B. Eerdmans, 2000 (reprint of *Naming the Silences: God, Medicine and the Problem of Suffering,* 1990).

Hick, John. *Evil and the God of Love.* Rev. ed. New York: Harper & Row, 1978.

Inbody, Tyron. *The Transforming God: An Interpretation of Suffering and Evil.* Louisville, KY: Westminster John Knox Press, 1997.

Jones, L. Serene. "Hope Deferred: Theological Reflections on Reproductive Loss (Infertility, Miscarriage, Stillbirth)." *Modern Theology* 17:2 (April 2001): 227–45.

Kushner, Harold S. *When Bad Things Happen to Good People.* New York: Schocken Books, 1989.

Levenson, Jon D. *Creation and the Persistence of Evil: The Jewish Drama of Divine Omnipotence.* San Francisco: Harper & Row, 1988.

Pinn, Anthony B. *Why Lord? Suffering and Evil in Black Theology.* New York: Continuum, 1995.

Riemer, Jack, ed. *Wrestling with the Angel: Jewish Insights on Death and Mourning.* New York: Schocken Books, 1995.

Ruether, Rosemary Radford. *Christianity and the Making of the Modern Family.* Boston: Beacon Press, 2000.

Sands, Kathleen M. *Escape from Paradise: Evil and Tragedy in Feminist Theology.* Minneapolis: Augsburg Fortress Press, 1994.

Sia, Marian F., and Santiago Sia. *From Suffering to God: Exploring Our Images of God in the Light of Suffering.* New York: St. Martin's Press, 1994.

Stimming, Mary T. "Crucifixion Amnesia: Left Out on Mother's Day." *The Christian Century* 114, no. 15 (May 7, 1997): 436–37.

_____. "Endless Advent?: Childless in December." *The Christian Century* 117 (December 6, 2000): 1273–75.

Walton, Heather. "Passion and Pain: Conceiving Theology out of Infertility." *Contact,* no. 130 (1999): 3–9.

Biblical Resources

Ackerman, Susan. "Child Sacrifice: Returning God's Gift: Barren Women Give Birth to Exceptional Children." *Bible Review* 9 (June 1993): 20–28, 56.

Blessing, Kamila. "Desolate Jerusalem and Barren Matriarch: Two Distinct Figures in the Pseudepigrapha." *Journal for the Study of the Pseudepigrapha* 18 (October 1998): 47–69.

Dresner, Samuel H. "Barren Rachel." *Judaism* 40 (Fall 1991): 442–51.

Mbuwayesango, Dora R. "Childlessness and Woman-to-Woman Relationships in Genesis and in African Patriarchal Society: Sarah and Hagar from a Zimbabwean Woman's Perspective (Gen.16:1–16; 21:8–21)." *Semeia,* no. 78 (1997): 27–36.

Pastoral Care and Grief Counseling

Brabant, Sarah. "'My Baby Had No Name': Women and 'Inappropriate' Grief." *Daughters of Sarah* 18, no. 4 (Fall 1992): 40–43.

Carter, Warren. "Miscarriage: Pastoral and Theological Perspectives." Unpublished master's thesis. Melbourne, Australia: Melbourne College of Divinity, 1986.

Case, Ronna. "When Birth Is Also a Funeral." *The Journal of Pastoral Care* 32, no. 1 (March 1978): 6–21.

Devor, Nancy Gieseler. "Pastoral Care for Infertile Couples." *The Journal of Pastoral Care* 48, no. 4 (Winter 1994): 355–60.

Dixon, Elizabeth Nimitz. "When Birth Means Death." *The Christian Ministry* 15, no. 4 (July 1984): 16–19.

Doka, Kenneth J., ed. *Disenfranchised Grief: Recognizing Hidden Sorrow.* New York: Lexington Books, 1989.

DuBose, J. Todd. "The Phenomenology of Bereavement, Grief, and Mourning." *Journal of Religion and Health* 36, no. 4 (Winter 1997): 367–74.

Fickling, Karl F. "Stillborn Studies: Ministering to Bereaved Parents." *The Journal of Pastoral Care* 47, no. 3 (Fall 1993): 217–27.

Furman, Erna P. "The Death of a Newborn: Care of the Parents." *Birth and the Family Journal* 5, no. 4 (Winter 1978): 214–18.

Gilbert, Kathleen R. "Religion as a Resource for Bereaved Parents." *Journal of Religion and Health* 31, no. 1 (Spring 1992): 19–30.

Grossoehme, Daniel H. "The Experience of Miscarriage: One Father's Reflections." *The Journal of Pastoral Care* 49, no. 4 (Winter 1995): 429–31.

Houck, Dawn Kyoko. "Coping with Miscarriage: Psychological and Spiritual Healing through Grief Work and Reconciliation Rituals." In *Creative Ministries in Contemporary Christianity*, ed. Perry LeFevre and W. Widick Schroeder, 61–76. Chicago: Exploration Press, 1991.

Hunt, Swanee. "Pastoral Care and Miscarriage: A Ministry Long Neglected." *Pastoral Psychology* 32, no. 4 (Summer 1984): 265–78.

Joensen, William M. "Being and Infertility: Bearing the Mystery." *Josephinum Journal of Theology* n.s. 4, no. 1 (Winter/Spring 1997): 46–55.

Kirkley-Best, Elizabeth, Kenneth Kellener, Sharon Gould, and William Donnelly. "On Stillbirth: An Open Letter to the Clergy." *The Journal of Pastoral Care* 36, no. 1 (March 1982): 17–20.

Kirkman, Maggie. "Infertile Women and the Narrative Work of Mourning: Barriers to the Revision of Autobiographical Narratives of Motherhood." *Narrative Inquiry* 13, no. 1 (2003): 243–62.

Lothrop, Hannah. *Help, Comfort and Hope After Losing Your Baby in Pregnancy or the First Year.* New York: Perseus Publishing, 1997.

Manning, Martha. *All Seasons Pass: Grieving a Miscarriage.* Notre Dame, IN: Sorin Books, 2000.

Moe, Thomas. *Pastoral Care in Pregnancy Loss: A Ministry Long Needed.* Binghamton, NY: Haworth Press, 1996.

Morgan, John H., and Rachel Goering. "Caring for Parents Who Have Lost an Infant." *Journal of Religion and Health* 17, no. 4 (October 1978): 290–98.

Morrow, Judy Gordon, and Nancy Gordon DeHamer. *Good Mourning: Help and Understanding in Time of Pregnancy Loss.* Dallas, TX: Word Publishing, 1989.

Parachin, Victor M. "Helping Families Survive Stillbirth." *The Christian Ministry* 22, no. 4 (July–August 1991): 19–20.

_____ . "Sudden Death." *Leadership* 16 (Fall 1995): 117–19.

Peterman, Janet S. "A Pastoral and Theological Response to Losses in Pregnancy." *The Christian Century* 104, no. 25 (9–16 September 1987), 750–53.

Rando, Therese A. *Grief, Dying, and Death: Clinical Interventions for Caregivers.* Champaign, IL: Research Press, 1984.

_____ . *Treatment of Complicated Mourning.* Champaign, IL: Research Press, 1993.

Seaton, Kathleen Lull. "A Grief Unobserved: Caring for Families Following Early Pregnancy Loss." *Word & World* 16, no. 1 (Winter 1996): 38–44.

Spring, Beth. *The Infertile Couple.* Colorado Springs: David C. Cook, 1987.

Stevenson-Moessner, Jeanne. *The Spirit of Adoption: At Home in God's Family.* Louisville, KY: Westminster John Knox Press, 2003.

Tucker, Karen B. Westerfield. "A Pastoral Response to a Silent Tragedy." *The Christian Ministry* 20, no. 1 (January–February 1989): 11–13.

Wassner, William J. "The Pastoral Dynamics of Miscarriage." *Pastoral Psychology* 40, no. 2 (November 1991): 113–21.

Liturgical Resources

Book of Blessings. Approved for Use in the Dioceses of the United States of America by the National Conference of Catholic Bishops and Confirmed by the Apostolic See. Collegeville, MN: Liturgical Press, 1989.

Book of Common Worship. Presbyterian Church. Louisville, KY: Westminster John Knox Press, 1993.

Geitz, Elizabeth Rankin, Marjorie A. Burke, and Ann Smith, eds. *Women's Uncommon Prayers: Our Lives Revealed, Nurtured, Celebrated.* Harrisburg, PA: Morehouse Publishing, 2000.

Landers, Bertha. *Through Laughter and Tears—The Church Celebrates: Rites of Passage and Pilgrimage in the Christian Church.* Scottsdale, PA: Mennonite Publishing House, 2001.

Norén, Carol M. *In Times of Crisis and Sorrow: A Minister's Manual Resource Guide.* San Francisco: Jossey-Bass, 2001.

Occasional Services: A Companion to the Lutheran Book of Worship. Minneapolis: Augsburg Publishing House, 1982.

The United Methodist Book of Worship. Nashville, TN: United Methodist Publishing House, 1992.

Stories and Rituals

Anderson, Herbert, and Edward Foley. *Mighty Stories, Dangerous Rituals: Weaving Together the Human and the Divine.* San Francisco: Jossey-Bass Publishers, 1998.

Anselment, Raymond A. "'A Heart Terrifying Sorrow': An Occasional Piece on Poetry of Miscarriage." *Papers on Language & Literature* 33, no. 1 (Winter 1997): 13–46.

Cardin, Nina Beth. *Tears of Sorrow, Seeds of Hope: A Jewish Spiritual Companion for Infertility and Pregnancy Loss.* Woodstock, VT: Jewish Lights Publishing, 1999.

Devor, Nancy Gieseler. "A Service for Isaac." *The Christian Century* 105 (April 20, 1988): 391.

Fritsch, Julie, with Sherokee Ilse. *The Anguish of Loss: Visual Expressions of Grief and Sorrow.* Maple Plain, MN: Wintergreen Press, Reissue, 1992.

Gamble, Elette, and Wilbur L. Holz. "A Rite for the Stillborn." *Word & World* 15, no. 3 (Summer 1995): 349–53.

Garrison, Greg. "A Different Kind of Mother's Day." *Presbyterians Today* 86, no. 3 (April 1996): 20–21.

Grossman, Susan. "Finding Comfort After a Miscarriage." In *Daughters of the King: Women and the Synagogue: A Survey of History, Halakhah, and Contemporary Realities,* ed. Susan Grossman and Rivka Haut, 284–90. Philadelphia: The Jewish Publication Society, 1992.

Guóth-Gumberger, Márta. "Buried Under a Mango Tree: Infertility and Faith." *Daughters of Sarah* 18, no. 4 (Fall 1992): 12–13.

Holub, Margaret. "A Cosmology of Mourning." In *Life Cycles: Jewish Women on Life Passages and Personal Milestones,* ed. Debra Orenstein, 341–51. Woodstock, VT: Jewish Lights Publishing, 1994.

Morey, Ann-Janine. "In Memory of Cassie: Child Death and Religious Vision in American Women's Novels." *Religion and American Culture* 6, no. 1 (Winter 1996): 87–104.

Pitock, Todd. "Dreaming of Michaela." *Tikkun* 11, no. 6 (November–December 1996): 54–57.

Ramshaw, Elaine J. *Ritual and Pastoral Care*. Theology and Pastoral Care Series. Philadelphia: Fortress Press, 1987.

_____ . "Ritual for Stillbirth: Exploring the Issues." *Worship* 62, no. 6 (November 1988): 533–38.

Selis, Allen. "Liberating Reproduction from Despair: A Kavanah for Conception in the Age of Infertility." *Tikkun* 14, no. 3 (May–June 1999): 31–32, 63.

Sha, Janet L. *Mothers of Thyme: Customs and Ritual of Infertility and Miscarriage*. Ann Arbor, MI: Lida Rose Press, 1990.

Speller, Lydia Agnew. "The Empty Womb." *The Christian Ministry* 24, no. 3 (May–June 1993): 7–9.

Turner, Elizabeth Zarelli, and Philip Turner. "Where the Children Can Dance." *Sojourners* 18 (August–September 1989): 27.

Wassner, William J. "Blowing the Shofar: Announcing the Presence of God on the Occasion of Miscarriage." *Encounter* 52, no. 4 (Autumn 1991): 357–66.

Weems, Ann. *Psalms of Lament*. Louisville, KY: Westminster John Knox Press, 1995.

Wolterstorff, Nicholas. *Lament for a Son*. Grand Rapids, MI: Wm B. Eerdmans, 1987.

CONTRIBUTORS

Nadine Pence Frantz is Professor of Theological Studies at Bethany Theological Seminary (Richmond, Indiana), the graduate school of theology for the Church of the Brethren. An ordained minister in the Church of the Brethren, Professor Frantz completed her undergraduate education at Manchester College, a master's degree at Bethany Theological Seminary, and a doctorate in theology at the University of Chicago. She has previously published articles in the area of theology and the visual arts and is mother of Bryan through adoption.

Serene Jones is Titus Street Professor of Theology at Yale Divinity School (New Haven, Connecticut). Ordained in both the Christian Church (Disciples of Christ) and the United Church of Christ, Professor Jones completed her undergraduate education at the University of Oklahoma and her master's and doctorate in theology at Yale Divinity School. Her most recent book is entitled *Feminist Theory and Theology: Cartographies of Grace* (Fortress Press, 2000), and she is mother of Charis by birth.

Kristen E. Kvam is Associate Professor of Theology at St. Paul School of Theology (Kansas City, Missouri), a seminary of the United Methodist Church. Active in the Evangelical Lutheran Church in America, Professor Kvam completed her undergraduate education at St. Olaf College, graduate studies at Yale Divinity School, and doctorate in theological studies at Emory University. She recently co-edited *Eve and Adam: Jewish, Christian, and Muslim Readings on Genesis and Gender* (Indiana University Press, 1999) and is mother of Ellen and Joshua by birth.

Linda A. Mercadante is B. Robert Straker Professor of Theology at The Methodist Theological School in Ohio (Delaware, Ohio). Ordained within the Presbyterian Church (USA), Professor Mercadante completed undergraduate studies at the American University, graduate studies at Regent College (Vancouver, British Columbia), and her doctorate in theology at Princeton Theological Seminary. Her most recent book is entitled *Victims & Sinners: Spiritual Roots of Addiction and Recovery* (Westminster John Knox Press, 1996), and she is mother of David by adoption.

Mary T. Stimming is an adjunct Assistant Professor of Theology at Dominican University (River Forest, Illinois). Active within the Catholic Archdiocese of Chicago, Professor Stimming completed her undergraduate studies at Georgetown University and her doctorate in theology at the University of Chicago. She has previously published a collaborative volume entitled *Before Their Time: Adult Children's Experiences of Parental Suicide* (Temple University Press, 1999) and is mother of Michael, Kathryn, Paul, and Elizabeth through adoption.

Index of Biblical Passages

Index

adoption, 16, 36, 43, 92–93
  cultural views of, 4, 33, 36
  as metaphor, 88–90, 93–94, 97,
    110 n.2
  narratives of, viii–ix, 2, 16, 33,
    43, 92
Aristotle, 3, 7
artificial reproduction technology
  See pregnancy
baptism, 42, 79–80
  Luther on, 78–82
Barthelot, Elizabeth, 6, 36
Bible, 9, 10, 34, 89, 95–96
  barren matriarchs, 34, 105 n.2
blood, 43–44, 48, 55–57
Bugenhagen, John, 72–73
Calvin, John, 19, 51, 71
childlessness, 4–6
  voluntary, ix, 4
Christ, 23, 28–30, 43, 91, 105 n.7
  and church, 90, 96, 98–99
  and suffering, 19, 24, 44
  See also crucifixion; Jesus;
    resurrection; Trinity
"Child of God," 7, 41–42, 88

church, 30, 83, 92, 93–98
  adoption metaphor, 88–90,
    93–94, 97, 110 n.2
  and family, 90–91, 93–94
  and reproductive loss, viii,
    8–9, 42, 49–51, 65
  See also reproductive loss
crucifixion, 24, 44, 61–63
death, 2, 24, 26–27, 30
  menstruation as, 43–44
  and miscarriage, 58–59
  and Trinity, 61–63
desire, 34–36, 91–92
envy, 36–41, 42
Eucharist, 33, 44, 99
feminism, 4, 7, 9, 50–51, 52
  and theology, 41, 103 n.10
God, 20, 28, 29, 40–41, 61
  anger towards, 9, 18, 82
  and creation, 19–21, 61, 91
  images of, 21, 44, 50
  and suffering, 10, 20, 28–30,
    43, 65, 76–77
  theory of divine retribution,
    53, 77–78